A History of the Canadian Dollar

by James Powell

This publication is also available in French.
La présente publication est aussi disponible en français.

December 2005

ISBN 0-660-19571-2
Cat. No. FB2-14/2005E

Printed in Canada on recycled paper.

Table of Contents

Acknowledgements i

Introduction ii

The First Nations (ca. 1600–1850) 1

New France (ca. 1600–1770) 3

British Colonies in North America:
The Early Years (pre–1841) 11

Currency Reforms (1841–71) 21

The Canadian Dollar under the
Gold Standard (1854–1914) 33

Canada off the Gold Standard (1914–26) 37

Back on the Gold Standard—Temporarily
(1926–31) 41

The Depression Years and the Creation of
the Bank of Canada (1930–39) 44

Canada under Fixed Exchange Rates
and Exchange Controls (1939–50) 53

A Floating Canadian Dollar (1950–62) 61

Return to a Fixed Exchange Rate
(1962–70) 66

Return to a Floating Rate
(June 1970–present) 71

Concluding Remarks 85

Appendix A: Purchasing Power of
the Canadian Dollar 88

Appendix B: Alternative Money 92

Appendix C: Charts 97

Bibliography 99

Index 105

Acknowledgements

Many persons helped to make this second edition possible. I would like to thank Mike Bordo, Pierre Duguay, Tiff Macklem, John Murray, and Larry Schembri for their helpful comments and suggestions. Special thanks go to Paul Berry, Chief Curator of the National Currency Collection, for his comments and assistance in choosing pieces to supplement the story and for providing captions. Additional thanks go to the museum staff, including David Bergeron, Rebecca Renner, Lisa Craig, and Gord Carter who worked with Paul to provide the excellent illustrations. Jennifer Devine and Debbie Brentnell from Library and Archives Canada were also extremely helpful in locating and processing some of the editorial cartoons used in this book. Lisette Lacroix, Joan Teske, Judy Jones, and Taha Jamal provided invaluable research and technical assistance. The superb French translation was done by Lyse Brousseau, Sylvie Langlois, Shirley-Ann Dulmage, Denyse Simard-Ebert, and Andréa Pelletier, supported by René Lalonde and Sylvie Morin who proofread the French and English texts.

Lastly, I would like to thank Publishing Services for pulling the project together in an incredibly short period of time. Jill Moxley and Lea-Anne Solomonian, supported by Eddy Cavé and Glen Keenleyside, edited the manuscript. Michelle Beauchamp provided the very creative layout, and Maura Brown the comprehensive index, while Darlene Fougere kept us all on track.

James Powell

Introduction

The history of Canada's money provides a unique perspective from which to view the growth and development of the Canadian economy and Canada as a nation. Building on an earlier edition, this expanded *History of the Canadian Dollar*, traces the evolution of Canadian money from its pre-colonial origins to the present day. Highlighted on this journey are the currency chaos of the early French and British colonial period, the sweeping changes ushered in by Confederation in 1867, as well as the effects of two world wars and the Great Depression.

The book chronicles the ups and downs of the Canadian dollar through almost 150 years and describes our dollar's relationship with its U.S. counterpart. It also examines the forces that led to the adoption of the dollar as our currency during the nineteenth century, instead of the pound, as well as the factors that led Canada to move from the gold standard in the 1920s, to the Bretton Woods system of fixed exchange rates in the 1940s and, ultimately, to a flexible exchange rate regime in 1970.

Finally, on the seventieth anniversary of the establishment of the Bank of Canada in 1935, at the height of the Great Depression, this book examines the formation of Canada's central bank and its ensuing quest for a monetary order that best promotes the economic and financial welfare of Canada. While its tactics have changed over the years, the Bank's enduring goal has been the preservation of confidence in the value of money through achieving and maintaining price stability.

Wampum belt
As early as the seventeenth century, Native peoples in northeastern North America used wampum belts to record significant events. In the absence of coinage, colonists used individual pieces of wampum as money.

The First Nations
(ca. 1600–1850)[1]

The word "Canada" is reputed to come from the Iroquois-Huron word *kanata*, meaning "village" or "settlement." It is thus fitting to begin the story of the Canadian dollar with "money" used by Canada's First Nations.[2] The Aboriginal peoples of eastern North America placed a high value on strings and belts fashioned from beads of white or purple shells found on the eastern seaboard. Early English settlers called such articles "wampum," an abbreviation of an Algonquin word sometimes spelled *wampumpeague*. French settlers called shell beads *porcelaine*.

Wampum was highly valued, partly because of the difficulty in making shell beads even after European tools became available in the seventeenth century. By one estimate, it took 119 days to make a 5,000-bead belt (Lainey 2004, 18). Strings and belts made from purple beads were roughly twice the value of those made from white beads, since the purple shell was much more difficult to work.

Wampum is particularly associated with the Iroquois nations and features prominently in the legends surrounding the formation of the Iroquois Confederacy. The use of shell beads by the Aboriginal peoples of the St. Lawrence River was described by Jacques Cartier in the sixteenth century and by Samuel de Champlain in the early seventeenth century.

Early Europeans viewed wampum as a type of money. A mid-seventeenth century observer writes,

> Their money consists of certain little bones, made of shells or cockles, which are found on the sea-beach; a hole is drilled through the middle of the little bones, and these they string upon thread, or they make of them belts as broad as a hand, or broader, and hang them on their necks, or around their bodies. They have also several holes in their ears, and there they likewise hang some. They value these little bones

---

1. This section draws heavily on Lainey (2004) and Karklins (1992).
2. Anything that is typically used as a medium of exchange to buy goods and services can be considered to be money. Other functions of money include serving as a store of value and a unit of account.

as highly as many Christians do gold, silver and pearls . . . (Reverend Johannes Megapolensis, Jr., 1644 in Karklins 1992, 67).

Wampum became an essential part of the fur trade as European settlers used shell beads to buy beaver pelts from the Iroquois and other inland peoples. Wampum had all the hallmarks of a useful currency. There was strong demand for it among the Native peoples, beads were difficult to make, and they were conveniently sized. Indeed, for a period during the mid-seventeenth century, wampum was legal tender in colonial New England, with a value of eight white beads or four purple beads to a penny (Beauchamp 1901, 351).[3] In 1792, legislation was passed in Lower Canada to permit the importation of wampum for trade with Native peoples.

While useful as a medium of exchange, the significance of wampum to the Aboriginal peoples of eastern North America far transcended its monetary role. Wampum had considerable symbolic and ritualistic value. In an oral society, the exchange of wampum helped convey messages and was used to cement treaties between Indian nations, as well as with Europeans. Wampum was also exchanged in marriages and funerals and used in spiritual ceremonies.

By the mid-nineteenth century, the exchange of wampum in diplomatic and other ceremonies had fallen into disuse, although there are reports of its use in Iroquois funeral ceremonies into the twentieth century (Lainey 2004, 82). The use of wampum for ceremonial purposes has been revived in recent years.

While shell beads were also valued on the west coast, copper shields were the ultimate symbol of wealth among the Haida people. High-ranking chiefs could own many shields, which were often exchanged at increasing values at potlach ceremonies.[4] Like wampum in the east, copper shields and other copper items were a key element in the culture of the peoples of the north-west coast. Haida symbols are featured on the 2004 $20 note, linking our heritage to the present.

Haida shield, nineteenth century
The copper shields used in the potlatch ceremonies of the west coast Native peoples represented wealth. Some of the largest pieces were highly valued and were even given names.

---

3. Legal tender money describes money that has been approved for paying debts or settling commercial transactions.
4. Canadian Museum of Civilization (2005).

New France
(ca. 1600-1770)

Trade silver, beaver, eighteenth century
Manufactured in Europe and North America for trade with
the Native peoples, trade silver came in many forms, including
ear bobs, rings, brooches, gorgets, pendants, and animal shapes.

According to Adam Shortt,[5] the great Canadian economic historian, the first regular system of exchange in Canada involving Europeans occurred in Tadoussac in the early seventeenth century. Here, French traders bartered each year with the Montagnais people (also known as the Innu), trading weapons, cloth, food, silver items, and tobacco for animal pelts, especially those of the beaver.

In 1608, Samuel de Champlain founded the first colonial settlement at Quebec on the St. Lawrence River. The one universally accepted medium of exchange in the infant colony naturally became the beaver pelt, although wheat and moose skins were also employed as legal tender. As the colony expanded, and its economic and financial needs became more complex, coins from France came to be widely used.

France, double tournois, 1610
Originally valued at 2 deniers, the copper "double tournois" was shipped to New France in large quantities during the early 1600s to meet the colony's need for low-denomination coins.

Because of the risks associated with transporting gold and silver (specie) across the Atlantic, and to attract and retain fresh supplies of coin, coins were given a higher value in the French colonies in Canada than in France. In 1664, this premium was set at one-eighth but was subsequently increased. In 1680, *monnoye du pays* was given a value one-third higher than *monnoye de France*, a valuation that held until 1717 when the distinction was abolished and all debts and contracts in Canada became payable in *monnoye de France*.

---

5.   This section draws heavily on Shortt (1925a, 1925b, 1986).

France, 15 sols, 1670
In an attempt to address perennial coin shortages in France's North American colonies, Louis XIV ordered the production of three denominations in 1670, including the "double d'amerique" (a base-metal coin), a 5-sol piece, and a 15-sol piece. The "double" was never issued, and the others proved unpopular since they could not be used to pay taxes.

Mexico, 8 reals, seventeenth century
Called "cobs" from the Portuguese *cabo* meaning "bar," these irregular-shaped coins, struck in silver cut from large ingots, were common in the European colonies of North America during the 1600s and early 1700s.

An inability to keep coins in circulation in French colonies in the Americas led to the minting in 1670 of silver and copper coins designed specially for the colonies.[6] These coins could not be circulated in France on pain of confiscation and punishment. While apparently intended primarily for the West Indies, a small number of these coins are believed to have circulated in Canada (Shortt 1986, 118).

Spanish dollars (*piastres*) also began to circulate in the French colonies during the mid-1600s owing to illegal trading with English and Dutch settlers to the south, who used them extensively. Because these coins were of uncertain quality, an "*arrêt*" of 1681 required that foreign coins be weighed. In 1683, foreign coins had to be individually appraised. Full-weighted Spanish dollars were stamped with a fleur-de-lys and were valued at four *livres*, while light coins, depending on their weight, were stamped with a fleur-de-lys and

a Roman numeral I, II, III, and IIII, with the lightest coin assigned a value of only 3 *livres*. Arguably, these overstamped Spanish dollars (and parts thereof) represent the first distinctive Canadian coins. They also foreshadowed the use of Spanish dollars in what was to become British North America.

The introduction of card money

In 1685, the colonial authorities in New France found themselves short of funds. A military expedition against the Iroquois, allies of the English, had gone badly, and tax revenues were down owing to the curtailment of the beaver trade because of the war and illegal trading with the English. Typically, when short of funds, the government simply delayed paying merchants for their purchases until a fresh supply of specie arrived from France. But the payment of soldiers could not be postponed. Having exhausted other

---

6.   The units of account in France at this time and in the French colonies in the Americas were *livres*, *sols*, and *deniers*. As was the case with English pounds, shillings, and pence, there were 20 *sols* to the *livre*, and 12 *deniers* to the *sol*. There were no *livre* coins. Other coins in circulation included the *louis d'or*, the *écu*, the *liard*, and the *double tournois*. Their values varied widely over time with changes in their gold or silver content, government policy, and inflation. For example, the value of the *louis d'or* ranged from 10 *livres* in 1640 to 54 *livres* in 1720 (McCullough 1984, 43).

financing avenues and unwilling to borrow from merchants at the terms offered, Jacques de Meulles, Intendant of Justice, Police, and Finance came up with an ingenious solution—the temporary issuance of paper money, printed on playing cards. Card money was purely a financial expedient. It was not until later that its role as a medium of exchange was recognized.

The first issue of card money occurred on 8 June 1685 and was redeemed three months later. In a letter dated 24 September 1685, to the French Minister of the Marine justifying his action, de Meulles wrote,

> I have found myself this year in great straits with regard to the subsistence of the soldiers. You did not provide for funds, my Lord, until January last. I have, notwithstanding, kept them in provisions until September, which makes eight full months. I have drawn upon my own funds and from those of my friends, all I have been able to get, but at last finding them without means to render me further assistance, and not knowing to what Saint to say my vows, money being extremely scarce, having distributed considerable sums on every side for the pay of the soldiers, it occurred to me to issue, instead of money, notes on cards, which I have cut in quarters . . . I have issued an ordinance by which I have obliged all the inhabitants to receive this money in payments, and to give it circulation, at the same time pledging myself, in my own name, to redeem the said notes (Shortt 1925a, 73, 75).

These cards were readily accepted by merchants and the general public and circulated freely at face value. Card money was next issued in February 1686. The authorities in France were not pleased, however. In a letter to de Meulles dated 20 May 1686, they wrote,

> He [His Majesty] strongly disapproved of the expedient which he [de Meulles] has employed of circulating card notes, instead of money, that being extremely dangerous, nothing being easier to counterfeit than this sort of money. Letter to de Meulles, 20 May 1686 (Shortt 1925a, 79)[7]

Notwithstanding this admonition, the colonial authorities reissued card money in 1690 because of another revenue shortfall. Again, the cards were redeemed in full. However, given their wide acceptance as money, a significant proportion was not submitted for redemption and remained in circulation, allowing the government to increase its expenditures. The following year, with yet another issue of card money, the Governor, Louis de Buade, Comte de Frontenac, acknowledged the useful role that card money played as a circulating medium of exchange in addition to being a financing tool (Shortt 1925a, 91).

While the authorities in France worried about the risk of counterfeiting and a loss of budgetary control, the colonial authorities successfully argued that the cards served as money

---

7.   The cards were, in fact, almost immediately counterfeited. See ordinance of de Meulles announcing the redemption of the card money, 5 September 1685 (Shortt 1925a, 73). If caught, the penalty for counterfeiting was severe; Louis Mallet and his wife Marie Moore were condemned to be hanged at Quebec on 2 September 1736 for counterfeiting card money (Shortt 1925b, 591).

in Canada just as coin did in France. Moreover, the Kingdom of France derived benefits from the circulation of cards, since the King was not obliged to send coins to Canada risking loss "either from the sea or from enemies." Reflecting the mercantilist sentiments of the time, they less cogently argued that if coins were to circulate in Canada, some would be used to buy supplies from New England, resulting in "considerable injury to France by the loss of its coinage and the advantage which it would produce among her enemies."[8]

The concerns of the authorities in France were not entirely misplaced. In the early 1690s, the first signs of inflation began to be noticed as a result of the excessive issuance of card money. Although cards continued to be redeemed in full upon presentation, the stock of card money increased over time faster than demand, causing prices to rise. With the finances of the French government progressively deteriorating during the first part of the eighteenth century, owing to European wars, financial support for its Canadian colonies was reduced. The colonial authorities in Canada consequently relied increasingly on card money to pay their expenses. In 1717, with inflation rising sharply, it was agreed that card money should be redeemed with a 50 per cent discount and withdrawn permanently from circulation. At this time, Canada also adopted the *monnoye de France*.[9]

French Regime, playing card money, 50 livres, 1714 (reproduction)
Playing cards inscribed with a value and signed by the governor of New France were Canada's first paper currency and circulated from 1685 to 1714. No genuine examples are known to exist.

French Regime, 9 deniers, 1722H
In another effort to meet the need for small change, the Compagnie des Indes authorized the production of 9-denier pieces, dated 1721 and 1722. These were struck at two mints: Rouen, designated by the mint mark "B" below the date, and Larochelle, indicated here by the letter "H."

8. Letter from the Sieur de Raudot, 30 September 1706 (Shortt 1925a, 157).
9. Acadia retained the *monnoye du pays* valuation for French coins until at least the mid-1740s (Shortt 1986, 169).

By failing to provide a replacement for card money, the unintended consequence of this monetary reform was recession. In an attempt to remedy the situation, copper coins were introduced in 1722, but they were not well received by merchants. Notes issued by private individuals based on their own credit standing also circulated as money, a practice that pre-dated this event, and continued periodically well into the nineteenth century and, arguably, even to the present day.[10] The government, again short of funds, also issued promissory notes called *ordonnances,* which began to circulate as money.

In March 1729, in response to requests from the public, the government received permission from the King to reintroduce card money. These cards would be redeemed each year for goods or for bills of exchange[11] drawn on funds appropriated for the support of the colony that would be payable in cash in France.[12] The cards, which were strictly limited, were legal tender for all payments and replaced the *ordonnances* in circulation.

Confidence in this new card money was initially high. With the supply limited and convertible into bills of exchange payable in France, the cards were an economical alternative to the transfer of specie across the Atlantic. Gold and silver began to accumulate in New France and stayed. The government, however, remained financially constrained and began to rely again on *ordonnances* and another form of Treasury notes called *acquits* to fund its operations.

With issuance tightly controlled, card money traded at a premium for a time as the government increased its issuance of Treasury notes to pay for its operations. But as French finances deteriorated and the redemption of Treasury notes was repeatedly postponed, trust in card money was also undermined.

French Regime, card money, 24 livres, 1729
Printed on playing card stock, the size and shape differed according to the denomination. This piece is signed by Governor Beauharnois, Intendant Hocquart, and Varin, the agent for the Controller of the Marine.

---

10. See *bons,* Appendix B.
11. Bills of exchange (similar to cheques) were commonly used to finance foreign trade.
12. See memorandum of the King to the Marquis de Beauharnois, Governor and Lieutenant General of New France, and Sieur Hocquart [Intendant], Commissary General of the Marine and Controller of the Currency, 22 March 1729 (Shortt 1925b, 583).

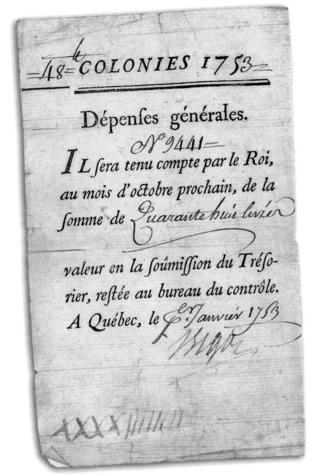

By the early 1750s, the distinction between card money and Treasury notes had largely disappeared, and by 1757, the government had discontinued payments in specie; all payments were made in paper. In an application of Gresham's Law—bad money drives out good—gold and silver were hoarded and seldom, if ever, used in transactions.

French Regime, ordonnance, 48 livres, 1753
Although there was a limit on the number of cards that could be issued, no such restriction existed for notes called *ordonnances*, issued by the Treasury in Quebec City. As a result, they were overissued, which contributed to a distrust of paper currency.

French Regime, bill of exchange, 1,464 livres, 1759
Issued by colonial officials at Quebec to pay the expenses of the colony, bills of exchange drawn on Paris were also endorsed and exchanged as a rudimentary form of paper money in New France.

A rapid increase in the amount of paper in circulation during the late 1750s resulting from the mounting costs of the war with the British, declining tax revenues, and rampant corruption, led to rapid inflation.

In a letter dated 12 April 1759, the Marquis de Montcalm noted that

> provisions absolutely necessary to life, cost eight times more than when the troops arrived in 1755. . . . The colonist is astounded to see the orders of the Intendant, in addition to the cards, circulating in the market to the extent of thirty millions. People, fear, I think without foundation, that the government will make a sort of assignment or authorize a depreciation. This opinion induces them to sell and speculate at an extravagant scale and price. . . . (Shortt 1925b, 889, 891).

On 15 October 1759, the French government suspended payment of bills of exchange drawn on the Treasury for payment of expenses in Canada until three months after peace was restored.[13] Paper money traded at a sharp discount. Immediately following the British conquest in 1760, paper money became all but worthless. But business in Canada did not come to a halt. Gold and silver that had been hoarded came back into circulation.

Gresham's Law

Gresham's Law, commonly described as the principle that "bad money drives out good," was attributed in the nineteenth century to Sir Thomas Gresham (1519–79), an English merchant and financier. In a letter to Queen Elizabeth I, after her accession in 1558, Gresham made this observation in reference to the poor state of English coinage owing to the debasement of the currency during the reigns of her predecessors. While often ascribed to Gresham, the principle had, in fact, been widely observed and commented on in much earlier times.

The idea behind the principle is that people will use "bad" money (e.g., debased coins or paper money) in payments, while "good" money (full-weight coins) is hoarded. However, Gresham's Law is frequently misunderstood. A more accurate rendition of the principle is that bad money drives out good money *if they are exchanged at the same price*. Such a situation would arise if both modes of payment are legal tender and therefore can be used equally to make payments. Moreover, good money can circulate alongside bad if the demand for money for transactions purposes is not fully satisfied by the circulation of bad money. As well, over history, strong currencies, from the Roman denarius to the U.S. dollar, have predominated in international trade over weak currencies because of widespread confidence in their quality and stability. See Mundell (1998) for an extensive review.

---

13. See "Suspension of payment of bills of exchange," Versailles, October 15, 1759 (Shortt 1925b, 929, 931). News of the suspension, which took until June 1760 to reach Canada, caused financial panic (Shortt 1925b, 941).

Settlement of the paper obligations issued by the colonial authorities in Canada was included in the Treaty of Paris, signed in February 1763, which ended the war between Great Britain and France.[14] In anticipation of a favourable settlement, speculators bought card and other paper money. British merchants also began to accept the paper, although at a discount of 80 to 85 per cent. Governor Murray, in charge of British troops in Quebec, recommended that Canadians hold onto their paper in the hope of a better deal.[15]

After extensive negotiations over the next three years, the French government finally agreed to convert card money and Treasury paper into interest-earning debentures on a sliding scale depending on the type of notes and their age, with discounts ranging from 50 per cent to 80 per cent. Typically, older notes were given a smaller discount. However, with the French government essentially bankrupt, these bonds quickly fell to a discount and, by 1771, they were worthless.

France, louis d'or, 1723
The French government routinely shipped specie (gold and silver coins) to New France. This piece was retrieved from the wreck of *Le Chameau*, which sank off the coast of Cape Breton near Louisbourg on 26 August 1725.

---

14. The great philosopher and economist, David Hume, who was the British Chargé d'Affaires in Paris at the time, played an active role in the negotiations dealing with the settlement of card and other paper obligations of the French government. See Dimand (2005).
15. See letter by Governor Murray, dated 14 February 1764 (Shortt 1925b, 993).

British Colonies in North America:
The Early Years (pre-1841)[16]

England, George III, guinea, 1775
The guinea was named after the area of Africa where the gold used for its production was first mined. The royal titles on the reverse are among the most lengthy on any British coin. Rendered in Latin, they read (George III by the grace of God) King of Great Britain, France and Ireland, Defender of the Faith, Duke of Brunswick and Luneburg, High Treasurer and Elector of the Holy Roman Empire.

Until the middle of the nineteenth century, each British colony in North America regulated the use of currency in its own jurisdiction.[17] Although pounds, shillings, and pence (the currency system used in Great Britain) were used for bookkeeping (i.e., as the unit of account), each colony decided for itself the value, or "rating," of a wide variety of coins used in transactions or to settle debts.[18] These included not only English and French coins, but also coins from Portugal, Spain, and the Spanish colonies in Latin America—notably Mexico, Peru, and Colombia. Once rated, coins became legal tender.[19]

Ratings were based on the amount of gold or silver contained in the coins and varied widely

Spain, 8 reals, 1779
This large silver coin, bearing a bust of King Charles III, was a Spanish colonial coin struck in Mexico. It was typical of the "silver dollars" that circulated in Canada and the United States.

from colony to colony but were always higher than the rating used in Great Britain. For example, in the mid-eighteenth century, a Spanish silver dollar, "the principal measure of exchange and the basis of pecuniary contracts" in North America, was appraised at 4 shillings and 6 pence in London, 5 shillings in Halifax, 6 shillings in New England,

---

16. This section draws heavily upon McCullough (1984). See also Shortt (1914a).
17. These comprised Upper and Lower Canada, New Brunswick, Prince Edward Island, Nova Scotia, Newfoundland and, later, Vancouver Island and British Columbia.
18. British colonies in North America were generally forbidden to mint their own coins.
19. Gold coins in circulation included Portuguese *johannes* and *moidores*, Spanish doubloons, English guineas, and French *louis d'or*. Silver coins included Spanish and colonial Spanish dollars (also called "pieces of eight," since a dollar was worth eight *reals*, or eight bits, with two bits equalling one quarter), British and French crowns, shillings, Spanish *pistareens*, and French 36- and 24-*sol* pieces. (See McCullough 1984.)

Great Britain, 1 shilling, 1825
The British shilling was widely used across British North America. As with other silver and gold coins of this period, its value was officially inflated to keep it from being sent out of the country.

Spain, 2 reals, 1760
Called the *pistareen*, this coin was widely used in British North America during the early nineteenth century because it was officially overvalued compared with similar-sized coins that had a higher silver content.

7 shillings and 6 pence in Pennsylvania, and 8 shillings in New York (Pennington 1848, 64). The higher colonial ratings reflected efforts to attract and retain specie (gold and silver) in the colonies to mitigate an apparent shortage of specie in circulation.

At times, colonial authorities also deliberately overrated (i.e., overvalued) or underrated (undervalued) certain coins relative to others in order to encourage or discourage their circulation. Ratings were also revised in response to other factors, including the decline in the value of silver relative to gold throughout the eighteenth and nineteenth centuries and the gradual wearing of coins, which lowered their weight and reduced their intrinsic value.

The reasons for a shortage of coin in the colonies are unclear. One view maintains that it reflected the perils of sea travel, as well as persistent trade imbalances with Britain. Another view argues that the shortage of money was more apparent than real, since trade was not the only source of specie, and paper alternatives were not considered. Moreover, colonial currency legislation encouraged the circulation of poor-quality coins. Overrated coins drove out underrated coins, which were hoarded, leaving light and poor-quality coins in circulation. Consequently, silver and gold coins of full weight could be obtained only at a premium, giving the impression of scarcity (Redish 1984).[20]

Not surprisingly, the wide variety of ratings among the British colonies in North America caused confusion and complicated trade. As a result, efforts were made to standardize ratings in order to facilitate commerce among the colonies and with Great Britain. As early as June 1704, Queen Anne issued a royal proclamation to remedy "the inconveniences which had arisen from the different rates at which the same species of foreign silver coins did pass in her Majesty's several colonies and

---

20. This view is supported by a contemporary writer. George Young, in his enquiry into colonial exchanges in 1838, makes reference to a pamphlet published in Boston in 1740, which stated, "In sundry of our colonies were enacted laws against the passing of light pieces of eight; these laws not being put into execution, heavy and light pieces of eight passed promiscuously, and as it always happens, a bad currency drove away the good currency—heavy pieces of eight were shipped off" (Young 1838, 38).

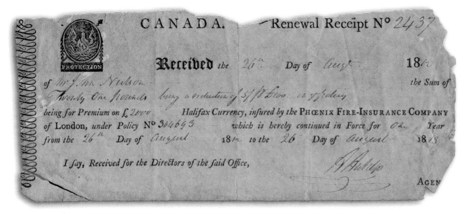

Phoenix Fire Insurance, receipt, 1812
Because of the multiple currency systems in North America at the beginning of the nineteenth century, businesspeople had to clearly define the system of account that they were using. This receipt was made out in "Halifax currency," under which 5 shillings were worth 1 dollar.

plantations in America." Under this proclamation, colonies were forbidden to rate a Spanish dollar any higher than 6 shillings. Because the proclamation was ignored, the British Government converted it into legislation in 1707 with stiff penalties for those who did not comply.[21] However, British colonies in North America and the Caribbean continued to ignore or evade the law, and business went on as usual.

The Halifax and York ratings

One rating that became particularly important in British North America was the Halifax rating. Named after the city of Halifax, where it was first used, this rating was given legal standing by an act of the first Nova Scotia House of Assembly in 1758 (Flemming 1921; McQuade 1976).[22] This rating used pounds, shillings, and pence ($£$, s., and d.) as the unit of account and valued one Spanish (or colonial Spanish) silver dollar weighing 420 grains (385 grains of pure silver[23]) at 5 shillings, local currency. This valuation of the Spanish dollar was to be used in settling debts. In effect, the Spanish dollar became legal tender in Nova Scotia.

Although the British imperial authorities apparently overturned the legislation in 1762 (Flemming 1921), the Halifax rating remained in common use in Nova Scotia and was later adopted in Quebec by the British authorities after the Seven Years' War, as well as in New Brunswick and Prince Edward Island.[24]

---

21.   An Act for Ascertaining the Rates of Foreign Coins in Her Majesty's Plantations in America
22.   The Halifax rating came into existence shortly after the founding of Halifax in 1749. It is reported that Governor Cornwallis bought silver dollars from a ship in Halifax harbour in 1750, paying 5 shillings each (Flemming 1921, 115). The Halifax rating was in general use by 1753 (Shortt 1933, 404).
23.   A grain is a measure of weight. Under the system used to weigh precious metals, there are 480 grains in a troy ounce.
24.   In 1765, the British military authorities introduced a Quebec rating, which valued the Spanish dollar at 6 shillings. This rating was dropped in 1777 in favour of the Halifax rating.

In contrast, following the U.S. War of Independence, Upper Canada used the York rating, as did merchants in Montréal, for a time. This rating had originally been established in New York and was brought to Upper Canada by Loyalist immigrants (Turk 1962). In York currency, one Spanish dollar was valued at 8 shillings.

In 1796, parallel legislation in both Upper and Lower Canada led to the adoption of the Halifax rating of 5 shillings to the dollar in both colonies, although ratings of other coins continued to differ to the inconvenience of trade between Upper and Lower Canada. Notwithstanding this legislation, the York rating remained in use in Upper Canada. In 1821, the legislature reaffirmed the colony's adoption of the Halifax rating and provided sanctions against the use of the old York rating. Nonetheless, there were reports of its continued use in rural areas until the unification of Upper and Lower Canada in 1841 (McCullough 1984, 92).

The lack of a standard currency, and the wide variety of ratings given to the many coins in general circulation in the colonies, undoubtedly hindered trade, and was a major source of economic inefficiency. But the prevalence of the practice suggests significant countervailing forces. These included the weight of custom, as well as the varying trade links among the colonies and with Great Britain. In addition, the implementation of a common rating would likely have led to winners and losers, as well as to deflation in those colonies required to reduce their ratings.

The introduction of paper money

As was the case in New France, British colonies in North America also experimented with paper money with mixed success, issuing "bills of credit." These bills, typically, although not exclusively, used as a means of wartime finance, were denominated in convenient amounts and circulated widely as currency. The Massachusetts Bay Colony was the first British colony in North America to issue such bills of credit in 1690. Paper money issued by Massachusetts, or "Boston bills," circulated in Nova Scotia during the first half of the eighteenth century owing to close economic and political links between Massachusetts and the British garrison and community in Annapolis Valley, formerly Port Royal (Mossman 2003).

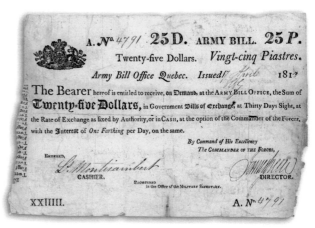

Army bill, $25, 1813
Printed in Quebec City, these notes were used to pay troops and to buy provisions during the War of 1812. At the end of the war, the bills were redeemed in full, which restored trust in paper money.

Bills of credit were not backed by specie and fell into disrepute because of overissuance and high inflation in the U.S. colonies prior to and during the American Revolution. Trust in paper money was restored in Upper and Lower Canada by a successful issue of army bills to help finance the War of 1812. The initial issue was for £250,000 worth of bills, denominated in dollars, by the government of Lower Canada; later issues raised the amount outstanding to £1.5 million. These bills were legal tender in both Upper and Lower Canada. Larger bills, those with a value of $25 or more, earned interest. By 1816, after the war ended, all bills had been redeemed in full (McArthur 1914, 505).

Island of St. John, 10 shillings, 1790
The Island of St. John, now known as Prince Edward Island, was one of the first colonies in British North America to issue Treasury notes.

Other provinces had broadly similar experiences. Prince Edward Island (then called the Island of St. John) experimented with paper money as early as 1790, when the colony issued £500 of Treasury notes to make up for a shortage of coin. These notes were legal tender and were issued in amounts of up to £2. Further issues followed through the first half of the nineteenth century.

In New Brunswick, the authorities issued Treasury notes on several occasions, first denominated in dollars in 1805 and 1807, and then in pounds following the War of 1812. The government discontinued such issues in 1820.

Nova Scotia also issued Treasury notes to help finance its military expenditures during the War of 1812. (See Martell 1941.) Although Nova Scotia was little affected by the war, the colonial authorities developed a taste for paper money as a means of financing public works and continued to issue new series of Treasury notes after the war. The first issue was interest-bearing and redeemable in specie at par. In time, however, the backing of the notes deteriorated, and by 1826, the notes had become inconvertible. The amount in circulation also increased dramatically over time.

Bank of Upper Canada, Kingston, $5, 1819
One of the earliest notes issued in Canada, this bill bears an early image of Fort Henry, built by the British to help secure the St. Lawrence waterway.

Bank of Upper Canada, York, $5, 1830
The Bank of Upper Canada was the first bank to conduct business at York, now Toronto. For most of its existence, it acted as the government bank for the Province of Upper Canada, before going bankrupt in 1866.

Initially, Treasury notes were well received by Nova Scotians and were used widely. But as their quantity increased and quality (i.e., their convertibility) decreased, they began to lose their value. In 1832, efforts were begun to establish a sound currency in Nova Scotia and to strengthen the credit standing of the province. The stock of outstanding Treasury notes was reduced, and in 1834, all private notes issued by banks, firms, and individuals were required to be redeemable in specie. This sharp monetary contraction exacerbated a serious economic downturn in 1834.

Some years later in 1861, the Colony of British Columbia issued Treasury notes, first seemingly in pounds and, subsequently, in dollars. These notes, which were used to finance public works, circulated freely, given a shortage of minted coins.[25]

Montreal Bank, $1, 1821
The Montreal Bank was chartered as the Bank of Montreal in 1822. This note is from a pre-charter issue produced by the American printer Reed Stiles and Company. The design features Britannia with a ship, the symbol of commerce, together with a representation of a city, perhaps Montréal. At the centre bottom is an image of a Charles IV Spanish dollar, an indication of value for those unable to read.

---

25. Gold dust was also used as a medium of exchange in the colonies of Vancouver Island and British Columbia following the discovery of gold in the Fraser River in the late 1850s. The use of gold dust was open to abuse, since the dust was of uncertain quality and had to be weighed (Reid 1926).

Government experiments with issues of paper money met with mixed success in both the French and British colonies in North America. Typically introduced to meet the exigencies of war, government-issued paper money was initially well accepted by the population and helped to facilitate commerce. But with few controls in place to limit the circulation of notes, the temptation of governments to rely increasingly on issues of paper to finance their operations often proved to be too great. Rapid increases in the stock of paper money relative to demand led to inflation, a growing reluctance to accept paper money at par with specie and, ultimately, the need for monetary reform.

The first bank notes

The first bank notes in Canada were issued by the Montreal Bank (subsequently called the Bank of Montreal), following its establishment in 1817.[26] These notes were issued in dollars. The success of the Bank of Montreal led to the incorporation of additional banks in Upper and Lower Canada as well as in the Atlantic provinces, all of which issued their own bank notes.[27] These included the Bank of Quebec in Quebec City and the Bank of Canada in Montréal, in 1818; the Bank of Upper Canada at Kingston, in 1819; the Bank of New Brunswick in St. John, in 1820; the Second or Chartered Bank of Upper Canada in

Bank of Nova Scotia, £5, 1820–1830s
This note is an example of an early chartered bank note. It was a "remainder" (i.e., it was never issued, as indicated by the holes punched across the bottom) and was printed in England.

Nova Scotia, 1 pound, 1831
As an anti-counterfeiting measure, the government of Nova Scotia issued Treasury notes during the 1820s and 1830s that were printed in blue ink rather than the more conventional black.

---

26. There are examples of notes, denominated in pounds and shillings, issued by the Canada Banking Company in 1792. It is not clear, however, whether this bank ever opened for business.

27. The charter of the Bank of Montreal, which provided the model for other Canadian banks, was itself modelled on that of the First Bank of the United States, which was established in 1791 by Alexander Hamilton, the first U.S. secretary of the Treasury (Shortt 1914a, 610).

York (Toronto), in 1822; the Halifax Banking Company, in 1825; the Bank of Nova Scotia in Halifax, in 1832; and the Bank of Prince Edward Island, in 1855.

Bank notes represented the principal liability of a bank and were redeemable in specie, upon demand. Banks committed themselves to maintain convertibility and, under their charters, restricted their total liabilities to a given multiple of their capital.[28] The extent of their note issues was also limited by the public's willingness to hold their notes. Unwanted notes were returned to the issuing bank and converted into specie.

Bank of New Brunswick, £1, 1831
The Bank of New Brunswick received its charter in 1820. This is a large-format note (184 mm by 98 mm), typical of the early notes issued by chartered banks.

Bank notes were well received by the public and became the principal means of payment in British North America. The general acceptance of bank notes in transactions helped to mitigate the problems associated with having a wide range of foreign coins in circulation with different ratings (Shortt 1986, 234).

As new banks were incorporated in Upper and Lower Canada during the 1830s and 1840s, their bank notes were typically denominated in both dollars and pounds. These notes circulated freely in both the Canadas and in the United States, although often at a discount, the size of which varied depending on distance, the name of the issuing bank, and the currency rating used.[29] Dollar-denominated bank notes issued by U.S. banks also circulated widely in Upper Canada during the early 1800s.

In contrast, bank notes circulating in New Brunswick, Nova Scotia, Prince Edward Island, and Newfoundland were typically denominated in pounds, shillings, and pence. This reflected both the stronger ties these provinces had with Great Britain and their weaker commercial links with the United States.

---

28. During periods of financial stress, convertibility was sometimes suspended.
29. During much of the nineteenth century, a bank's notes had to be accepted at par only at the issuing office. Elsewhere, the notes were discounted, even by branches of the issuing bank (Shortt 1914b, 279).

Dollars and cents or pounds, shillings, and pence?

As noted earlier, pounds, shillings, and pence were used as the unit of account in the British colonies of North America up until the middle of the nineteenth century. Given the scarcity of British coins, however, and the prevalence and wide acceptance of Spanish silver dollars, it became increasingly difficult to maintain a currency system based on sterling. The introduction of the U.S. dollar (modelled on the Spanish dollar)

in the United States in 1792, together with growing trade and financial links between Upper and Lower Canada and the United States during the first half of the nineteenth century, also favoured the use of dollars. The same was true for the colonies of Vancouver Island and British Columbia on the west coast, with the preponderance of their trade being with San Francisco during the late 1850s and early 1860s.

United States, half-dollar, 1827
During the early 1800s, the American half-dollar was imported by Canadian banks and used widely in Upper and Lower Canada. Workers on the Rideau Canal were paid with these pieces.

William IV half-crown, 1836
This is an example of British coinage used in the mid-nineteenth century. A half-crown was worth 2 shillings and 6 pence, or 50 cents.

Canadian bank notes, denominated in dollars, were also widely accepted and circulated freely in the United States. Had Canada adopted the sterling standard, this circulation would have the British Empire based on pounds, shillings, and pence. The British authorities believed that an empire-wide common currency would strengthen economic and political ties. In a letter to Sir James Kempt, the Governor General, dated 6 February 1830, which was subsequently tabled in the House of Assembly of Lower Canada, Sir Randolph Routh, the Commissary General of the British forces in the Canadas, stated,

> The British Government have in view the political tendency of this introduction of English money into the Colonies. A similarity of coinage produces reciprocal habits and feelings, and is a new chain and attachment in the intercourse of two nations. (Journal of the House of Assembly, Lower-Canada 11 George IV, Appendix Q, 9 March 1830).

Despite such pressure from the British Government, local custom and practices dominated. There was also a first-mover problem. While Nova Scotia was willing to adopt sterling, it would do so only if neighbouring colonies did so as well. Colonial co-operation was, however, not forthcoming (Martell 1941, 18).

Adam Shortt noted,

> To the eye of pure reason the scheme [a common imperial currency] was faultless. Even official minds trembled on the verge of sentiment in contemplation of its vast imperial possibilities. But, unfortunately, the shield had another side, the colonial, from which it excited little enthusiasm. Hence, in the course of the official attempts to put the ideal in practice, it encountered the most unlooked for obstacles and caused no little bitterness (Shortt 1986, 223).

been lost, to the detriment of Canadian banks (Shortt 1986, 428).

The widespread use and popularity of the dollar, combined with the potential cost of shifting to a sterling standard, stymied efforts by the imperial authorities in British North America to establish a common monetary system throughout

Great Britain, sovereign, 1817
The image of St. George and the dragon, which appears on the reverse of this coin, was engraved by the famous Italian medallist Benedetto Pistrucci, who later became Chief Medallist (1828–55) at the Royal Mint in London.

Currency Reforms
(1841-71)

Political union of Upper and Lower Canada to create the Province of Canada on 10 February 1841 led to a new standardized rating for coins in the newly united province that took effect in April 1842.[30] The British gold sovereign was valued at one pound, four shillings, and four pence in local currency, while the US$10 gold eagle was valued at two pounds, ten shillings.[31] Both coins were considered legal tender. Spanish (including Spanish colonial) and U.S. silver dollars with a minimum weight of 412 grains were also made legal tender with a value of five shillings and one pence—a valuation very similar to the old Halifax rating.

At this time, efforts also began to move to a decimal-based currency system and to introduce a government issue of paper currency. In 1841, Lord Sydenham, Governor General of the new united Province of Canada, proposed that the

United States, $10, 1844
Called an "eagle," after the prominent image appearing on the reverse, this coin was occasionally used in Canada for large transactions.

provincial legislature establish a provincial bank that would issue up to £1 million in provincial paper currency denominated in dollars, 25 per cent of which would be backed by gold, the remainder by government securities. He also recommended that notes issued by chartered banks be prohibited. In effect, Lord Sydenham's proposal amounted to the establishment of a Canadian central bank.[32]

---

30. In addition to McCullough (1984), this section draws heavily from Breckenridge (1910) and Shortt (1914b).
31. Recall that colonial legislatures rated coins higher than in Great Britain, where a sovereign was worth £1 sterling. The valuation for the U.S. gold eagle is for coins minted after 1834. Coins minted before that date had a higher gold content and were worth £2 13s. 4d. each in local currency.
32. While perhaps the best-articulated proposal, this was not a new idea in Canada. As early as 1820, an anonymous pamphlet published in Quebec had advocated the establishment of a government-owned national bank that would be the sole issuer of paper money. See "Anonymous" (1820). The issue was also debated periodically in the assemblies of both Upper and Lower Canada.

While Lord Sydenham sought a paper currency with guaranteed convertibility, he was also strongly motivated by a desire to acquire funds to finance provincial public works and to obtain the seigniorage profits from the note issue. Seigniorage was estimated to be at least £30,000 per annum and had the potential to rise considerably as the currency issue increased (Breckenridge 1910).[33]

The proposal was studied by a parliamentary select committee on banking and currency, headed by Francis Hincks, who strongly favoured the Governor General's plan. The provincial assembly turned it down, however, because of widespread opposition, particularly from a strong bank lobby. Banks were concerned about the impact on their profits if they lost the right to issue paper currency. Interestingly, borrowers were also worried that government control of the bank note issue would lead to tighter credit conditions. There were also concerns that the government would gain too much power. Because of the assembly's rejection of the Governor General's proposal, a provincial issue of paper currency had to wait another 25 years. The establishment of a central bank was delayed almost 100 years.

Upon Confederation in 1867, there was another proposal to make the new federal government the sole issuer of legal tender paper money, with the seigniorage accruing to the government. Unlike the earlier Sydenham proposal, the money would be fiat-based; i.e., inconvertible into gold. Moreover, there was no specific reference to the establishment of a bank. Instead, control of the proposed new monetary system would be given to a small number of commissioners, of whom the minister of finance would be an *ex officio* member. In apparent recognition of the potential perils of giving such authority to the government, ties to the government would be restricted to the minister of finance (Davis 1867). While this proposal did not succeed, it foreshadowed key elements of modern central banking—a fiat currency, a government monopoly on the issuance of paper money, and independence for the issuer.[34]

Introduction of a decimal-based currency

Despite Lord Sydenham's failure to introduce a government issue of paper currency, efforts to introduce a decimal-based currency in British North America gained momentum through the 1850s, especially during the government of Francis Hincks, who became prime minister of the Province of Canada in 1851. In June of that year, representatives from the Province of Canada, New Brunswick, and Nova Scotia met in Toronto to work towards the establishment of a decimal currency. A few months later, the Canadian legislature passed an act requiring that provincial accounts be kept in dollars and cents. However, the British government, still seeking to establish a

---

33. Seigniorage arises from the fact that the province would issue non-interest-bearing paper money while earning interest on the securities backing the currency issue. These profits would otherwise have been earned by banks on their issue of notes.

34. This paper foreshadowed a movement during the 1870s, headed by Isaac Buchanan, a wealthy Hamilton merchant and politician, aimed at introducing an inconvertible, government-issued paper money (Helleiner 2003, 88).

currency system based on pounds, shillings, and pence throughout the empire, delayed confirmation of the act on a technicality. While willing to concede the introduction of a decimal currency, the British government was still reluctant for Canada to adopt the dollar—the currency system of a foreign government with possible continental ambitions. Instead, the British authorities proposed the introduction of the "royal," a gold coin linked to sterling, with subsidiary silver and copper coins, to be called "shillings," and "marks," respectively. While Hincks was open to the idea, this proposal was rejected by the legislature (Shortt 1914b, 276).

A compromise Currency Act was finally passed in 1853 and proclaimed on 1 August 1854. Under this act, pounds, shillings, and pence, as well as dollars and cents, could be used in provincial accounts and were recognized as units of Canadian currency.

The Currency Act also confirmed the ratings of the British sovereign and the US$10 gold eagle that had been in place since the establishment of the Province of Canada in 1841. The British gold sovereign was rated at £1 4s. 4d. local currency or Can$4.8666, while the gold eagle (those minted after 1834 with a gold content of 232.2 grains) was valued at Can$10. British coins, both gold and silver, as well as U.S. gold coins, were legal tender. Other foreign silver coins, while not legal tender, continued to circulate (McCullough 1984, 110).

Since the colonial authorities in New Brunswick had passed similar currency legislation in October 1852, the proclamation of the Currency Act in the Province of Canada meant that the two regions had compatible currencies, fixed at par with their U.S. counterpart, with $1 equivalent to 23.22 grains of gold (or $20.67 per troy ounce).

Province of Canada, double-proof set, 1858
To celebrate Canada's new coinage, several sets of specially struck coins, called proofs, were prepared for presentation.

Decimalization received a further boost a few years later. Following a recommendation from the public accounts committee, the Province of Canada revised the Currency Act in 1857 so that, from 31 December 1857, all provincial accounts would be kept in dollars. Silver and bronze coins, denominated in cents and bearing the word "Canada," were subsequently issued for the first time in 1858.[35] This marked the birth of a distinctive Canadian currency.

In Nova Scotia, decimalization occurred on 1 July 1860. Nevertheless, because the colony rated the sovereign at $5 instead of $4.8666, its currency remained incompatible with that of Canada and New Brunswick. New Brunswick officially decimalized on 1 November 1860, while Newfoundland passed similar legislation in 1863.[36] Like Nova Scotia, Newfoundland's currency was not compatible with that of Canada or New Brunswick. The colony of Vancouver Island decimalized in 1863, followed by British Columbia in 1865.[37] Manitoba decimalized in 1870, upon its entry into Confederation, and Prince Edward Island followed in 1871.

The first government note issue

In the late 1850s and the early 1860s, efforts were renewed in the Province of Canada to

Nova Scotia, 1 cent, 1861
Although Nova Scotia ordered its first coinage in 1860 to be ready for issue later that year, the Royal Mint did not ship the coins until 1862, owing to the heavy demand for domestic British coinage.

New Brunswick, 1 cent, 1861
Like Nova Scotia, New Brunswick did not receive its shipment of new decimal coins until 1862, almost two years after they were ordered.

Newfoundland, 20 cents, 1865
As a separate colony of the British Empire, Newfoundland had its own distinctive coinage, from 1865 to 1947.

---

35. Prior to the establishment of the Ottawa Mint in 1908 (a branch of the Royal Mint under the Imperial Coinage Act of 1870), coins used in Canada were minted in the United Kingdom. The first gold coins minted in Canada were sovereigns, identical to those produced in the United Kingdom except for a small identifying "C." It was not until May 1912 that the Ottawa Mint began to produce limited quantities of gold $5 and $10 coins. The Ottawa Mint became the Royal Canadian Mint in 1931.

36. The legislation took effect at the beginning of 1865.

37. The colonies of Vancouver Island and British Columbia were united in November 1866 under the name British Columbia. A decimal currency act for the new combined province was passed in 1867. British Columbia entered Confederation in 1871.

Bank of Montreal, 25 shillings or $5, 1852
This note is an example of the dual currency system that existed in the Province of Canada prior to decimalization in 1858.

Bank of Clifton, $5, 1859
This note was issued by an early Canadian chartered bank, which was also known as the Zimmerman Bank. It became a "wildcat" bank, issuing large quantities of notes with no intention of redeeming them. The detailed engraving is typical of nineteenth-century bank notes. The coloured "Five" is an anti-counterfeiting device.

introduce a government issue of paper money.[38] This time, the financial and political environment was more receptive than had been the case in 1841.

The collapse of a number of banks during this period brought bank notes issued by chartered banks into disrepute. In 1859, two Toronto-based banks, the Colonial Bank and the International Bank, failed. This was soon followed by the collapse of the Bank of Clifton and the Bank of Western Canada. The failures of these last two banks were particularly scandalous, with the former pretending to redeem its notes in Chicago and the latter, owned by a tavern-keeper, attempting to circulate worthless bank notes in the U.S. Midwest. In his authoritative review of early banking in Canada, Roeliff Breckenridge wrote,

No great loss was caused to the Canadian public by their collapse, but the scandal and the ease of acquiring dangerous privileges which had led to the scandal, called forth bitter and general complaint (Breckenridge 1910, 71).

Nevertheless, a loss of confidence in chartered bank notes, the principal means of payment, posed a threat to economic prosperity. To restore confidence in the currency and to raise funds for the government, in 1860 A.T. Galt, Finance Minister of the Province of Canada, proposed replacing chartered bank notes with an issue of government notes.[39] Once again, the chartered banks objected strongly to the potential loss of their bank-note-issuing privileges, and the proposal was quickly withdrawn. In 1866, however,

---

38. During 1848–49, the provincial government issued provincial debentures, which circulated in small denominations. They were interest earning and payable one year after issue, although the government could choose to reissue them. Arguably, these debentures set the stage for the subsequent issuance of provincial notes.

39. In contrast to Lord Sydenham's earlier proposal, the notion of establishing a provincial bank to issue the notes was dropped. Instead, a provincial Treasury department would be established that would issue the paper money.

Bank of Montreal, $5, legal tender note, 1866
Once the Bank of Montreal agreed to act as the government's banker in 1866, all of its note issues were overprinted to indicate government issue until newly designed provincial notes were received.

Province of Canada, $2, 1866
Produced by the British American Bank Note Company, which had offices in Montréal and Ottawa, this note was payable in Toronto.

with the Canadian government again seriously short of resources, the need for a new source of funding became acute.[40] Domestic and British banks were unwilling to advance new funds or roll over existing loans. Moreover, the provincial government was unable to sell bonds in London even at very high rates of interest. With all funding avenues apparently closed, the provincial authorities passed controversial legislation to issue up to $8 million in legal tender, provincial notes. These notes were payable on demand in gold in either Toronto or Montréal and were partly backed by gold—20 per cent for the first $5 million and 25 per cent for amounts in circulation in excess of $5 million. The Provincial Notes Act received royal assent on 15 August 1866.

Unlike Galt's earlier proposal, chartered banks were not obliged to give up their right to issue bank notes although they were encouraged to do so.[41] Compensation was offered, including the payment of 5 per cent of their average notes in circulation and a further 1 per cent per year for issuing and redeeming provincial notes. Nevertheless, only the Bank of Montreal, the government's fiscal agent, took up the offer. It too resumed its bank note issue following the passage of the 1871 Bank Act.

Confederation

Confederation on 1 July 1867 brought sweeping changes to banking and currency legislation in the provinces of Canada, Nova Scotia, and New Brunswick. Under the British North

---

40. This shortage partly reflected support given to the failing Bank of Upper Canada, the government's agent (until the end of 1863). The Bank of Upper Canada lost heavily on loans extended to the Grand Trunk Railway. In 1861, because of the tight links between the government, the bank, and the railway, the government agreed to maintain a minimum deposit of $1.2 million in the bank. The bank failed in 1866, with government losses amounting to about $1.3 million (Shortt 1914b, 289).

41. Chartered banks were required to give up their own note issues in order to acquire the right to issue provincial notes on behalf of the government.

Dominion of Canada, $1, 1870
Printed by the British American Bank Note Company and featuring a portrait of Jacques Cartier, this was part of the first series of notes engraved for the new Dominion. These notes were redeemable at the Office of the Receiver General in Ottawa or at the branch indicated on the back.

America Act, the government of the new Dominion was given jurisdiction over currency and banking. The Dominion Notes Act came into effect the following year. Under this legislation, the Dominion took over the various provincial note issues. Provincial notes issued in the Province of Canada were renamed "Dominion notes" and were made redeemable in Halifax and Saint John in addition to Montréal and Toronto. The Dominion Notes Act was subsequently extended to cover Prince Edward Island, Manitoba, British Columbia, and the Northwest Territories.

Like earlier provincial notes, Dominion notes were partly backed by gold. The first $5 million issued were 20 per cent backed, and the next $3 million, 25 per cent backed. Over time, the size of the authorized note issue was increased. There were also some changes to the percentage of notes backed by gold. By 1913, the first $30 million had a 25 per cent gold backing.[42] Issues in excess of $30 million had to be fully backed by gold.

Interestingly, although Dominion notes became redeemable in Halifax in 1868, Nova Scotia retained its own currency until April 1871, when the Dominion government passed the Uniform Currency Act.[43] At that time, Nova Scotian currency, which was still rooted in the old Halifax rating, was converted into Canadian currency at a rate of 75 Nova Scotian cents to 73 Canadian cents.[44]

The Uniform Currency Act also established that denominations of Canadian currency would be dollars, cents, and mills (a mill equalled one-tenth of a cent). Moreover, the Canadian dollar's value was fixed in terms of the British sovereign at a rate of $4.8666 and the US$10 gold eagle at a rate of $10—the same rates established in the 1853 Currency Act.

---

42. Legally, the 25 per cent reserve could be held in the form of gold or guaranteed debentures. In fact, the reserve was held entirely in the form of gold.
43. The Dominion government circulated a special issue of $5 notes in Nova Scotia, with the legend PAYABLE AT HALIFAX/ONLY printed vertically on them. These notes, issued in Nova Scotian currency, were worth only $4.86 in the rest of Canada (Haxby 1975).
44. There was considerable opposition to this change in Nova Scotia, given its continuing strong links to Great Britain. In Nova Scotian currency, a sovereign had conveniently been worth $5 instead of $4.8666 (Flemming 1921, 132). Newfoundland's currency was also not compatible with that of Canada. The Newfoundland dollar was worth roughly $1.014 Canadian dollars. Newfoundland's currency was made consistent with Canada's in 1895 (McCullough 1984, 223). The colony entered Confederation in 1949.

Bank of Montreal, $4, 1871
In the late nineteenth century, banks regularly featured images of their senior officers on their notes. Pictured on the left is R.B. Angus, General Manager (1869–79), and on the right, E.H. King, President (1869–73).

United States, half-dollar, 1859
Images representing Liberty figured prominently on American coins during the nineteenth century. Here, Liberty is a young woman seated and holding a staff topped with a Phrygian cap, a symbol of freedom, with a shield at her side emblazoned with the stars and stripes and a sash reading "Liberty."

The Dominion government also passed the Bank Act in 1871, which repealed all provincial acts that were in conflict with federal jurisdiction over currency and banking. Consequently, chartered banks in the four provinces eventually came under common regulation.[45] Chartered banks were allowed to issue notes with a minimum denomination of $4 (raised to $5 in 1880). Although banks, as a matter of course, held substantial reserves of Dominion notes and gold, they were not required to secure their note issues either by gold or by specific collateral. Note issues could not, however, exceed a bank's paid-in capital.[46] (Under the 1880 Bank Act revision, notes in circulation became a first lien on the issuing bank's assets in the event of failure.[47]) The government preserved the issuance of smaller notes for itself. It also issued notes in larger denominations to be used mainly for transactions between banks.

The silver nuisance and a question of copper[48]

During the mid-nineteenth century, U.S. silver fractional coins—dimes, quarters, and half-dollars—circulated freely in Canada, alongside British shillings and, after 1858, Canadian coins minted by the Province of Canada. U.S. coins in

---

45. Banks chartered before Confederation continued to operate under their provincial charters until those charters expired. They subsequently received federal charters.

46. This was modified in 1908 to allow banks to increase their notes in circulation beyond the usual limits (on a temporary basis) during the harvest season. In the 1913 revision of the Bank Act, banks were allowed to issue notes in excess of their paid-in capital, provided that the excess note issue was secured by gold or by Dominion notes (Beckhart 1929, 381).

47. Under the 1890 Bank Act, a Bank Circulation Redemption Fund was established by the government to give added protection to bank notes in case of insolvency. Banks maintained an amount equivalent to 5 per cent of their average annual circulation of notes in the fund and received 3 per cent interest. Banks were also required to establish redemption offices for their notes across the country. This meant that, for the first time, a bank's notes were circulated throughout the country without a discount (Helleiner 2003, 126).

48. This section draws on Weir (1903), Shortt (1914b), McCullough (1984), and Esler (2003).

circulation increased significantly during the U.S. Civil War (1861–65), as U.S. Army agents used silver to purchase Canadian grain and cattle to supply the Union Army. A substantial brokerage business also flourished, with Canadian brokers importing large quantities of fractional U.S. silver coins.

Initially, the U.S. silver, while not legal tender in Canada, was well received because of a shortage of small coins for small transactions; day-to-day transactions typically involved amounts less than one dollar.[49] Canadians also preferred the U.S. silver quarter over the Canadian 20-cent piece issued in 1858, given their familiarity with U.S. coinage. But, although U.S. coins were accepted at par by individuals and merchants, their bullion value was approximately 2.5 per cent less than their face value.[50] Consequently, as the amount of U.S. silver coins in circulation began to increase, banks either refused to accept them or accepted them only at a discount. The acceptance of U.S. silver coins at par by merchants and individuals but only at a discount by banks was a considerable nuisance, especially for merchants. They were, nonetheless, willing to tolerate the practice because of competitive pressures, the customary acceptance of U.S. coins at par, and the lack of an acceptable alternative. This problem was largely confined to the Province of Canada—Ontario and Quebec—since the Atlantic colonies had passed a law valuing U.S. coins at only 80 per cent of their face value.

20-cent or 25-cent coin?

In 1858, the Province of Canada issued silver coins in denominations of 20 cents, 10 cents, and 5 cents, in addition to 1-cent bronze coins. The *Toronto Leader*, a newspaper linked to the government, argued that a 20-cent coin was a logical choice since it was consistent with the Halifax shilling, and five Halifax shillings equalled one dollar. The newspaper also contended that a 25-cent coin was just a "convenience of habit" and was not a necessary feature of a decimal coinage. Regardless, Canadians disliked the 20-cent coin since it was easily confused with the similar-sized U.S. quarter. William Weir noted, "I never heard what fool in the Finance Department suggested the twenty cent piece, for in spite of the special pleading of the *Leader*, everyone saw it was a mistake . . ." (Weir 1903, 135–136). The 20-cent piece was withdrawn from circulation after Confederation and replaced by a Canadian quarter, first minted in 1870 (Weir 1903, 164; see also Cross 2003, 52).

---

49.   During the 1860s, a dollar had considerable purchasing power. See Appendix A, page 88, on the purchasing power of the Canadian dollar.
50.   In 1853, the U.S. government reduced the silver content of its fractional (i.e., less than one dollar) silver coins (McCullough 1984, 111).

William Weir, 1823–1905

Born in Greenden, Scotland in 1823, William Weir emigrated to Canada in 1842. He initially worked as a teacher near Lachute, Quebec, and, after learning French, moved to Montréal to work in a large wholesale and retail business. In 1847, Weir struck out on his own, first as a commission merchant and later as an exchange broker. Moving to Toronto in 1856, Weir came to prominence as publisher and editor of the *Canadian Merchants' Magazine*. He also became an early proponent of protection for Canadian maufacturers, a policy later adopted by the Conservative Party under the leadership of Sir John A. Macdonald and known as the *National Policy*. Weir returned to Montréal in 1859 and operated the brokerage firm Weir and Larminie. Weir is best known for his involvement, along with Sir Francis Hincks, in dealing with the "silver nuisance" in 1870. Weir later became vice-president of the Banque Jacques Cartier. In 1881, he became general manager and cashier of the Banque Ville-Marie. In July 1899, the Banque Ville-Marie failed because of fraudulent lending by Weir to himself and his friends. Even after its closure, the Bank continued to issue bank notes. With notes the first charge on the Bank's assets, note holders were well protected from loss. Depositors, however, received only 17 1/2 cents on the dollar. Total losses amounted to roughly $1.5 million. Weir was subsequently prosecuted and went to jail for two years. It took a jury just 15 minutes to convict him. (See Turley-Ewart 1999; Breckenridge 1910; Rudin 1985; and Weir 1903.)

With the discount on silver relative to gold widening in the mid-1860s, there were appeals to Parliament to do something. In 1868, the new Dominion government exported $1 million worth of U.S. silver coins to New York through the Bank of Montreal. But this move was insufficient. The following year, William Weir, an important Montréal financier, exported a further $2 million. Weir assumed the market risk associated with a possible adverse move in the price of silver, as well as the costs and risks associated with transporting the silver to market in New York. In 1870, Weir, backed by merchants, negotiated a deal with Sir Francis Hincks, the Dominion Finance Minister, to eliminate the remaining U.S. coins circulating in Canada. Despite considerable resistance from brokers who stood to lose business, it was agreed that banks would purchase and collect the unwanted silver coins, paying for them largely with their own bank notes. They would also receive a small commission from the government, as well as a government deposit of up to $100,000. The government assumed the transportation costs and market risks of exporting and selling the coins for gold. In total, the government shipped to New York and to London slightly more than $5 million in coins, sold at a discount of 5 to 6 per cent, at a net cost of roughly $118,000. Weir himself exported a further $500,000 in U.S. silver coins, as well as a considerable amount of overrated British silver coins that were also in circulation (Weir 1903, 159–160).

Weir tea service, 1880
In recognition of his efforts to help remove depreciated American silver coins from circulation in Canada, William Weir was presented with this sterling tea service in 1880. Manufactured by R. Hendery, a prominent silversmith in Montréal, it incorporates various silver coins and is part of the National Currency Collection, Bank of Canada.

Dominion of Canada, 25-cent fractional note, 1870
Although created to facilitate the removal of depreciated American silver from circulation before the arrival of the Dominion's first coinage in 1870, the shinplaster became popular and was issued until the end of the century.

The government took immediate steps to replace the foreign coins with an issue of Canadian silver coins in denominations of 50 and 25 cents that would be legal tender in amounts up to $10, as well as issues of $1 and $2 notes. As a temporary expedient to supplement the coin issue and meet the needs of commerce, the government also issued 25-cent "shinplasters,"[51] redeemable in gold. To ensure that depreciated U.S. silver did not flow back into Canada, the government also passed legislation stating that after 15 April 1870, U.S. silver coins were legal tender in Canada at a 20 per cent discount, a rate far below their bullion value.

After settling the silver nuisance, the government turned its attention to the reorganization of Canada's copper coinage, which was also in disarray. Prior to Confederation, Nova Scotia, New Brunswick, and the Province of Canada had all issued small-denomination copper coins, as did Newfoundland. However, large quantities of token copper pennies issued by banks based on the old pre-decimal system were still in general circulation. A wide range of European and U.S. copper coins also circulated freely, along with private tokens issued by merchants or individuals, and even brass buttons (Weir 1903, 161).

---

51. The term "shinplaster" dates back to the late seventeenth century when notes issued by the Continental Congress during the American Revolution were redeemed at only a fraction of their face value. Soldiers reputedly used them as insulation or dressings for wounds.

In 1870, at the prompting of Weir, Hincks authorized the government to accept bank-issued pennies and halfpennies as 2 cents and 1 cent, respectively, in amounts up to 25 cents, and encouraged banks and the general public to do the same (Weir 1903, 164). It was not until 1876 that the Dominion of Canada issued its own 1-cent coin (Cross 2003, 53).

The removal of U.S. and British silver coins from circulation in Canada, along with the reorganization of Canada's copper coinage, did much to promote the circulation of a distinctive Canadian currency.

Dominion of Canada, 5, 10, 25, and 50 cents, 1870
The Dominion of Canada's first coinage consisted of these four denominations. It was modelled on the provincial issue of 1858. One-cent coins were not ordered until 1876, since there were still adequate numbers of provincial cents on hand.

The Canadian Dollar under the Gold Standard (1854-1914)

Canada, $10, 1912
Although Newfoundland issued gold coins as early as 1865, the Dominion of Canada did not do so until 1912–14, when the recently established Royal Mint in Ottawa struck $5 and $10 pieces. When the redemption of Dominion notes into gold was suspended at the beginning of the First World War, the production of Canadian gold coins ceased.

Operation of the gold standard

From 1 August 1854 when the Currency Act was proclaimed, until the outbreak of World War I in 1914, the Province of Canada, and subsequently the Dominion of Canada, was continuously on a gold standard. Under this standard, the value of the Canadian dollar was fixed in terms of gold and was convertible upon demand. It was also valued at par with the U.S. dollar, with a British sovereign valued at Can$4.8666. As noted earlier, both U.S. and British gold coins were legal tender in Canada.

With the gold standard in place, monetary policy was largely "on automatic pilot." Paper money was freely convertible into gold without restriction, and there were no controls on the export or import of gold. This implied that there was virtually no scope for the authorities to manage the exchange rate or to conduct an independent monetary policy.[52]

Fluctuations in market exchange rates between the Canadian dollar and the U.S. dollar and the pound sterling, respectively, around their official values were generally limited by the gold "export" and "import" points. These points marked the exchange rates at which it was profitable for individuals to take advantage of price differences between the market and official exchange rates through the export and import of gold from the United States or the United Kingdom. The difference between the export and import points and the official rates reflected the cost of

---

52. Note, however, that following Confederation, the amount of Dominion notes issued without 100 per cent gold backing was increased over time from $8 million in 1868 to $30 million by 1913 (Beckhart 1929, 294). Rich (1988) argues that the marked expansion of the uncovered note issue through the 1867–85 period suggests that the government relied extensively on discretionary monetary policy during this time. After 1885, however, although the amount of Dominion notes in circulation continued to rise, there was a matching increase in gold reserves. Consequently, the percentage of gold reserves to Dominion notes in circulation rose from only 21 per cent in 1890 to 81 per cent at the outbreak of World War I (Rich, 71–73 and Beckhart, 296).

insuring and shipping gold to and from New York or London and Montréal, Canada's financial centre at that time. Given the proximity of New York, the margins against the U.S. dollar were very narrow around parity with a gold export point of Can$1.0008 and a gold import point of Can$0.9992. The margins around the $4.8666 par value of the pound sterling were somewhat wider, ±1 per cent, given the greater distance to be travelled (Rich 1988). On rare occasions, the Canadian dollar traded outside the gold points for periods of several weeks, much longer than one would have expected if arbitrageurs were efficient. This suggests that obstacles, probably imposed by governments in an effort to protect their gold reserves, might have impeded their activities (Turk 1962). While not a particularly significant phenomenon prior to 1914, government-erected impediments to the cross-border flow of gold became common during World War I and even more so through the late 1920s and early 1930s in order to conserve the country's gold reserves.

With monetary policy essentially on autopilot and little in the way of active fiscal policy, there was nothing to buffer economic swings and the impact of large international capital movements. In his 1867 pamphlet arguing in favour of government-issued fiat currency, Robert Davis contended,

> Such a currency, moreover, freed from the constraint of convertibility at the bank counter, would not be subject to the fluctuations to which our present circulation is constantly liable, and the injury to trade from its contraction, at the time its extension was most needed, would no longer exist . . . (Davis 1867, 32).

The price-specie flow

Classical economists explained international economic adjustment under the gold standard using a theory developed in part by David Hume—the price-specie flow. Under this theory, an economic shock that led to increased demand in one country, and rising prices, would trigger an increase in imports and a countervailing outflow of specie to the rest of the world. The drain in gold from the country experiencing the shock would reduce the quantity of money in that country, leading to higher domestic interest rates (which, in turn, would slow demand), lower prices (relative to those elsewhere), and higher exports. Increased net exports and capital inflows attracted by relatively high domestic interest rates would restore equilibrium to the balance of payments. The opposite process would happen simultaneously in the rest of the world. The successful functioning of this adjustment mechanism depends critically, however, on the sensitivity of demand to price changes in the countries affected. If the "price-elasticity of demand" was low, it would be possible under the fractional gold standard that prevailed during this period for a country's reserves of specie to be exhausted before adjustment was completed. See Yeager (1976).

This opposition remained a minority position, however, with the weight of orthodox economic views and conventions in support of the gold standard prevailing until the 1930s. Accordingly, Canada experienced booms and busts during the gold-standard years. For example, between 1870 and 1900, Canada suffered several economic contractions with falling prices. In contrast, between 1900 and 1913, Canada grew rapidly, and inflationary pressures mounted as huge amounts of foreign capital (as a percentage of Canadian GDP) entered the country. (See also Appendix A.)[53]

The Canadian dollar and the U.S. greenback (1862–79)

In 1862, the American Civil War began to affect currency in the United States. As the finances of the Union government deteriorated, U.S. banks suspended the convertibility of their notes into gold, and the government suspended the right to convert U.S. Treasury notes (government-issued paper money) into gold. Shortly afterwards, the U.S. Congress authorized the government to issue non-convertible legal tender currency, which became popularly known as "greenbacks." While little was said officially regarding the future convertibility of greenbacks into gold, it was widely assumed that convertibility would be restored when the war was won (Willard et al. 1995). Trading in the greenback vis-à-vis gold commenced in mid-January 1862 in New York and continued with

United States, $1, 1862
Known as the "greenback" and produced during the Civil War, this was part of a note issue that re-established a government (paper) currency in the United States.

only one short interruption until the United States returned to the gold standard on 1 January 1879.

Almost from the start of trading, the greenback depreciated relative to gold and against other currencies, including the Canadian dollar, which remained on the gold standard. The weakness in the greenback undoubtedly reflected the rapid expansion of the U.S. note issue from $150 million in early 1862 to $450 million by March 1863. Fluctuations in its value also reflected the military and political fortunes of the Union government and, hence, the expected likelihood

---

53. Net capital inflows into Canada reached a record 18 per cent of GDP in 1912 (Urquhart 1986).

that the government would eventually be able to redeem the greenbacks in gold. The greenback tended to strengthen on news of Union victories, such as the Battle of Gettysburg in 1863, and weakened on Union reversals. It reached its nadir during the summer of 1864, when the Union government, in a move against speculators, temporarily shut down gold trading for two weeks in late June, followed in early July by Confederate advances towards Baltimore and Washington and raiding operations in Pennsylvania.[54] Based on available information, the U.S. greenback fell from close to parity against the Canadian dollar in early 1862 to less than 36 Canadian cents (or Can$1=US$2.78) on Monday, 11 July 1864 (Chart 1).[55] This represents the all-time peak for the Canadian dollar in terms of its U.S. counterpart.

The greenback subsequently began to recover, almost doubling in value by the end of the Civil War in April 1865. After the war, it continued to strengthen, albeit at a slower pace, as the government retired a significant amount of greenbacks during the 1866–68 period. Deflation after the Civil War enabled the United States to return to the gold standard on 1 January 1879, with the greenback convertible into gold at the old pre-war rate of 23.22 grains of gold (Yeager 1976). Once again, the Canadian dollar traded at par with its U.S. counterpart. This exchange rate held until the outbreak of World War I.

Chart 1
Canadian Dollar in Terms of the U.S. Dollar
Monthly averages (1861–79)

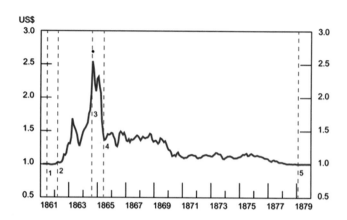

*11 July 1864: Can$1=US$2.78
1. April 1861: Outbreak of U.S. Civil War
2. January 1862: U.S. suspends gold convertibility.
3. June, July 1864: Closure of Gold Room, Confederate army approaches Washington.
4. April 1865: U.S. Civil War ends.
5. January 1879: U.S. returns to gold standard.
Source: Turk (1962), *Montreal Gazette*

---

54. Confederate troops led by Jubal Early came within five miles of the White House on 11 July 1864 before breaking off the raid and returning to Virginia (Willard et al. 1995, 17).
55. Exchange rate data were obtained from the *Montreal Gazette* on file at Library and Archives Canada.

Canada off the Gold Standard (1914-26)

Canada, Victory Bond, $100, 1915
This bond issue demonstrated that Canada had come of age financially.
It was oversubscribed entirely by Canadians, so that, for the first time,
Canada was able to offer Britain a loan for the purchase of war supplies.

World War I

The beginning of World War I marked the end of the classical age of the gold standard.[56] All major countries suspended the convertibility of domestic bank notes into gold and the free movement of gold between countries. This was often done unofficially. For example, in the United Kingdom, private exports and imports of gold remained legal in theory. However, in addition to a number of government-imposed regulations that discouraged the buying and selling of gold, bullion dealers refused to permit gold exports on patriotic grounds (Yeager 1976, 310).

In Canada, convertibility was officially suspended. As tensions mounted in the days immediately prior to the declaration of war on 4 August 1914, there were heavy withdrawals of gold from banks. In an "atmosphere of incipient financial panic" (Macmillan Report 1933, 22), there were concerns about the possibility of bank runs. In the absence of a lender of last resort, this was potentially very serious, since banks were legally required to close if they were not able to meet depositor demand for gold or Dominion notes.

On 3 August 1914, an emergency meeting was held in Ottawa between the government and the Canadian Bankers Association to discuss the crisis. Later that day, an Order-in-Council was issued that provided protection for banks that were threatened by insolvency by making notes issued by the banks legal tender. This allowed the banks to meet their depositor demands with their own bank notes rather than with Dominion notes or gold.

---

56. Although gold had been used as money since antiquity, a fully fledged international gold standard lasted a surprisingly short time—roughly 40 years. It was not until the 1870s that a gold standard was finally adopted in all major economies (Yeager 1976, 295).

Home Bank, $10, 1917
The Home Bank was one of several chartered banks established in Canada during a period of economic expansion early in the twentieth century. Its operations were suspended in 1923, owing to poor management. Following a Royal Commission into its operations, the Office of the Inspector General of Banks (the forerunner of the Office of the Superintendent of Financial Institutions) was established in 1925.

The Finance Act gave the government the power to act as a lender of last resort to the banking system—one of the powers of a modern central bank. It also provided a means for the government (Treasury Board) to set the Advance Rate, the rate at which it would make loans to the chartered banks. (See Chart C2 in Appendix C.) Advances under the Finance Act were made at the request of banks. The government did not actively manage interest rates, nor was there any board overseeing the conduct of monetary policy (Shearer and Clark 1984, 279).

The government also increased the amount of notes that banks were legally permitted to issue. The government was also empowered to make advances to banks by issuing Dominion notes against securities deposited with the minister of finance. This provision enabled banks to increase the amount of their bank notes in circulation.

A second Order-in-Council, issued on 10 August 1914, suspended the redemption of Dominion notes into gold. This and the previous Order-in-Council were subsequently converted into legislation as "An Act to Conserve the Commercial and Financial Interests of Canada" (the Finance Act), which received royal assent on 22 August 1914.

Chart 2
Canadian Dollar in Terms of the U.S. Dollar
Monthly averages (1914–26)

1. August 1914: Outbreak of World War 1
2. November 1918: End of World War 1
3. July 1926: Return to gold standard
Source: U.S. Board of Governors of the Federal Reserve System (1943)

Dominion of Canada, $2, 1914
The portraits of Canada's Governors General and their wives were commonly featured on Canadian government notes in the late nineteenth and early twentieth centuries. The Duke of Connaught, Governor General from 1911 to 1916, and his wife are shown here.

Dominion of Canada, $1, 1917
This note features Princess Patricia, daughter of the Duke and Duchess of Connaught and patron of the famous Princess Patricia's Canadian Light Infantry.

Throughout the war, the Advance Rate remained at 5 per cent, although a special 3.5 per cent rate was established in 1917 under which the government discounted British treasury bills held by the chartered banks. This facility was designed to assist the British government's war effort. It was complemented by a special $50 million issue of Dominion notes backed by British treasury bills to help finance British purchases of war materials in Canada (Macmillan Report 1933, 22). The government also increased the fiduciary issue of Dominion notes (i.e., notes not backed by gold)

in 1915 under an amendment to the Dominion Notes Act.

Despite the suspension of gold convertibility in August 1914, the Canadian dollar traded in a very narrow range close to parity with its U.S. counterpart throughout the war years (Chart 2). In 1918, however, the Canadian dollar began to weaken, and its decline accelerated during the two-year period following the end of hostilities, until it reached a low of roughly US$0.84 in 1920. The weakness of the currency reflected a significant monetary expansion, high inflation, and a deterioration in Canada's balance of payments associated with financing the war effort and the ensuing cost of troop demobilization (Shearer and Clark 1984, 282; Knox 1940).

Setting the stage for a return to the gold standard

There was a general presumption that, after the war, the major industrial countries would return to the gold standard. The United States, which was a late entrant into the war and did not experience the same sort of financial or inflationary pressures as the United Kingdom or Canada, returned to its old fixing in terms of gold in June 1919. The United Kingdom controversially followed suit in 1925 at its old pre-war price in terms of gold, equivalent to US$4.8666.[57]

In Canada, the Finance Act of 1914, which had been adopted as a war measure, was extended in 1919 and revised in 1923. Under the revised act, provision was made for an automatic return to the gold standard after three years unless the government took steps to the contrary.

The revised act also gave the Dominion government greater flexibility to adjust the rate at which banks could obtain funding.[58] However, the Treasury Board, which was responsible for administering the act, did not conduct an active monetary policy.

The Advance Rate remained fixed at 5 per cent, the same level it had been throughout the war. Thus, there appeared to be little overt official effort to tighten monetary policy in anticipation of an eventual return to the gold standard, which would fix the dollar at its pre-war value in terms of gold and at par with its U.S. counterpart.

Despite the apparent lack of action, the money supply did contract significantly during the first half of the 1920s, permitting a return to the gold standard. The maintenance of the Advance Rate at 5 per cent, despite a fall in market interest rates, had deflationary consequences. (See Chart A2 in Appendix A.) Moreover, Britain's repayment of war loans from Canadian banks (which were subsequently discounted under the Finance Act at the special 3.5 per cent rate) and the retirement of the so-called "British Issue" of Dominion notes issued in 1917 against British treasury bills also contributed to the monetary contraction (Shearer and Clark 1984, 291). Expansionary monetary policy in the United States, partly aimed at facilitating the return of European countries to the gold standard, also facilitated Canada's return to the gold standard on 1 July 1926. However, gold reserves were widely viewed as inadequate to the task (Bryce 1986, 36).

---

57. John Maynard Keynes famously opposed this move in a pamphlet entitled "The Economic Consequences of Mr. Churchill." Given a relatively high rate of inflation in the United Kingdom during and immediately following the war, the old pre-war parity for sterling was seen as being too high. Efforts to sustain the pound at its pre-war rate led to a serious recession and deflation.

58. Under the 1914 act, the Advance Rate could not fall below 5 per cent. This minimum level was removed in the 1923 revision.

Back on the Gold Standard—Temporarily (1926-31)

Canada, $5 and $10 patterns, 1928
Following the resumption of the gold standard in 1926, consideration was briefly given to striking $5 and $10 gold pieces similar to those issued prior to World War I. Copper patterns were prepared, but no further action was taken.

With Canada's return to the gold standard, currency supplied by the chartered banks lost its legal tender status, although the government could restore this status under the Finance Act in the event of an emergency. Consequently, legal tender in Canada once again consisted of British gold sovereigns and other current British gold coins, U.S. gold eagles ($10), double eagles, and half eagles, Canadian gold coins (denominations of $5 and $10), and Dominion notes. Limited legal tender status was also accorded silver, nickel, and bronze coins minted in Canada.[59]

Canada's return to the gold standard proved to be short-lived. It has been argued that monetary operations under the Finance Act were inconsistent with maintaining a gold standard. Dominion notes issued to banks under the authority of the act upon the pledge of securities were not backed by gold.[60] They were, however, legally redeemable in gold on demand. In 1933, James Creighton, a prominent University of British Columbia economics professor, wrote,

> Apparently the sponsors of the 1923 Act did not realize that when Canada went back on the gold standard, as she did in 1926, the effects of the operations of the Act would be vitally different from what they were during the paper money period (Creighton 1933, 116).

Some modern-day economists also point to excessive monetary expansion during the late 1920s as causing the eventual demise of the gold standard (Courchene 1969, 384). The percentage of gold reserves to Dominion notes outstanding

---

59. Silver coins were legal tender in amounts not exceeding $10; nickel coins in amounts not exceeding $5; and bronze coins in amounts not exceeding 25 cents (Macmillan Report 1933, 37).

60. Limits were set annually for advances to chartered banks under the Finance Act. Because they were typically set very high, such limits did not pose an effective restraint on the borrowing activities of banks.

fell from 54 per cent on 30 June 1926 to 28 per cent three years later (Macmillan Report 1933, 38). Other economists have emphasized the unwillingness of the Canadian authorities to accept the discipline of the gold standard, especially during a period of significant international financial stress (Shearer and Clark 1984, 300). A fall in commodity prices, resulting in a deterioration in Canada's trade balance, was also a factor. The currencies of other heavily indebted, commodity-producing countries, such as Australia and Argentina, also came under significant downward pressure during the 1929–31 period (Knox 1940, 8).

The Canadian dollar experienced three bouts of weakness between 1928 and 1931. But instead of automatically allowing the export of gold when the dollar weakened beyond the gold-export point, as it would have done under a "pure" gold standard, the government increasingly relied on a number of "gold devices" to stop its export (Shearer and Clark 1984, 29–30). For example, instead of making gold available in Montréal or Toronto as required by law, it was available only in Ottawa, thereby increasing the cost and inconvenience of exporting gold. Similarly, instead of supplying U.S. gold coins, the authorities provided British sovereigns or bullion, which had to be assayed before the U.S. authorities would accept it. Alternatively, only small-denomination coins were provided. Moral suasion was also used on bullion shippers.

An increase in the Advance Rate would have been the expected monetary response to the outflow of gold. While the "ordinary rate" was increased from 3.75 per cent to 5 per cent on 9 June 1928, a special 3.75 per cent rate remained in effect. To facilitate the sale of a special issue of 4 per cent treasury notes, the government had apparently made a commitment to the banks to discount these notes at this special rate (Shearer and Clark 1984, 295). When the pressure on the Canadian dollar temporarily eased in the autumn of 1928 because of seasonal factors, the ordinary Advance Rate was reduced to 4.5 per cent. It stayed at this level until late October 1931, despite the Canadian dollar falling below the gold-export point during late 1929 and early 1930 and again through the summer of 1931.

Banque Canadienne Nationale, $50, 1925
Based in Montréal, the Banque Canadienne Nationale issued a series of notes in 1925 that featured familiar Canadian statuary. The design of the $50 note included a portrait of the bank's President, J.A. Vaillancourt, the bank's General Manager, Beaudry Leman, and an image of the statue of Maisonneuve in Place d'Armes square in old Montréal.

In effect, if not in form, Canada went off the gold standard in 1929. However, the export of gold was not officially banned until 31 October 1931 by an Order-in-Council. The banks and the government also used moral suasion, through appeals to patriotism, to convince Canadians not to convert Dominion notes into gold (Bryce 1986). But with the politically traumatic, although economically sound, decision by the United Kingdom to abandon the gold standard on 21 September 1931, the fiction of a gold standard was finally abandoned.

With the pound sterling falling precipitously from its old fixed rate of US$4.8666 to as low as US$3.40 in the days immediately following the British decision to float the currency, the Canadian dollar came under sharp downward pressure (Chart 3) amid a general loss of confidence in the global financial system. World money markets essentially ceased to function, with borrowers, such as Canada, unable to borrow even short-term money in New York. Investor concern about Canada focused on the wavering nature of Canada's commitment to the gold standard, its high level of debt, and its low gold reserves (Creighton 1933, 122). In this environment, the Canadian dollar fell to a low of roughly US$0.80 in the autumn of 1931 before recovering.

The *coup de grâce* to Canada's adherence to the gold standard was finally delivered on 10 April 1933 when an Order-in-Council officially suspended the redemption of Dominion notes for gold.

As was the case in other countries that left the gold standard during the 1930s, this move was expected to be temporary, with a return to the gold standard widely anticipated once the economic climate improved (Bordo and Kydland 1992).

Chart 3
Canadian Dollar in Terms of the U.S. Dollar
Monthly averages (1926–39)

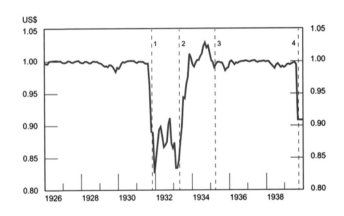

1. October 1931: Gold exports banned
2. April 1933: Redemption of Dominion notes into gold suspended
3. March 1935: Bank of Canada begins operations.
4. September 1939: War is declared, the Canadian dollar is fixed, and exchange controls are imposed.
Source: U.S. Board of Governors of the Federal Reserve System (1943)

Bank of Canada, $25, 1935
This note is the first commemorative note issued by the Bank of Canada. It was issued on 11 May 1935 to mark the 25th anniversary of the reign of King George V.

The Depression Years and the Creation of the Bank of Canada (1930–39)

Despite mounting evidence that a major economic contraction was under way following the stock market crash in October 1929, the federal government took little in the way of monetary action to support the economy.[61] Admittedly, the scope for policy action was constrained, since advances under the Finance Act were made at the initiative of banks, and there was no money market. Also, Canada was, at least notionally, still on the gold standard. Nonetheless, the government set the Advance Rate, and chose to hold it unchanged at 4.5 per cent from September 1928 to October 1931. As a result, questions were widely voiced regarding Treasury Board officials' understanding of monetary issues.

In his 1933 book on central banking in Canada, James Creighton argued that J. C. Saunders, Deputy Minister of Finance during the 1920s and *ex officio* Secretary of the Treasury Board, which administered the Finance Act on behalf of the Minister of Finance, was not competent in monetary matters. Creighton noted that Saunders and other deputy ministers had "neither an academic training in economics nor practical experience in banking." Moreover, the position of deputy minister was left vacant after Saunders' death for an extended and critical period—April 1930 to November 1932—leaving a serious policy vacuum (Creighton 1933, 86–90).

---

61. At the height of the Depression in 1933, real output in Canada had fallen by roughly 28 per cent from its 1929 level, while prices, as measured by the GDP deflator, had declined by about 15 per cent. Canadian exports had fallen by almost two-thirds from their 1928 peak.

Coincidentally, Benjamin Strong, Governor of the New York Federal Reserve since its establishment in 1914 and dominant personality in the Federal Reserve system during its formative years, died in October 1928. His death also left a policy vacuum in the United States at a critical time.

There is considerable controversy about Strong's policies and what would have happened had he lived. Some argue that his expansionary policies during the mid-1920s encouraged the speculative excesses that led to the stock market crash. Others contend that, had he lived, Strong would have moved quickly to moderate the effects of the Depression (Roberts 2000). Nonetheless, the Federal Reserve Bank of New York acted more quickly and aggressively to cut interest rates than did the Canadian government. The Fed's Discount Rate, the equivalent of the Canadian Advance Rate, was cut from 6 per cent at the time of the stock market crash in 1929 to 2 per cent by December 1930 (Chart C2 in Appendix C).[62]

At the same time that the Canadian government was doing nothing on the monetary front, the chartered banks were repaying their borrowings from the government under the Finance Act.[63] The resulting monetary contraction exacerbated the economic downturn. The banks became increasingly cautious about their own lending activities as the economic environment deteriorated. Banks may have also repaid their borrowings under the Finance Act in response to earlier criticism for having borrowed so extensively prior to the stock market crash (Fullerton 1986, 36).

While the extent of the economic downturn in Canada was undoubtedly made worse by these monetary developments, the monetary contraction helped to strengthen the Canadian dollar, which reached US$0.90 by the spring of 1932.

The government finally reduced the Advance Rate to 3 per cent in October 1931 and to 2.5 per cent in May 1933. (See Chart C2 in Appendix C.)[64] In the autumn of 1932, it also used moral suasion to force the banks to borrow under the Finance Act and reflate the economy (Bryce 1986, 132). This easing in monetary policy led to some temporary weakness in the Canadian dollar, which briefly fell as low as US$0.80. The weakness was short-lived, however. Following the U.S. decision to prohibit the export of gold in April 1933 and similar efforts in the United States to reflate, the Canadian dollar began to strengthen.[65] The Canadian government's decision in 1934 to expand the amount of Dominion

---

62. The Discount Rate at other Federal Reserve Banks was typically higher than that of the Federal Reserve of New York through the 1930s.

63. Advances under the Finance Act, which had peaked at $112.9 million in November-December 1929, fell to nil by the spring of 1931 (Macmillan Report 1933).

64. The Advance Rate was temporarily increased to 3.5 per cent from May 1932 to May 1933. However, special rates of 2.5 to 3 per cent were available on advances secured by certain securities.

65. The U.S. government subsequently re-fixed the U.S. dollar on 31 January 1934, such that one ounce of gold was worth US$35, compared with the pre-1933 price of US$20.67.

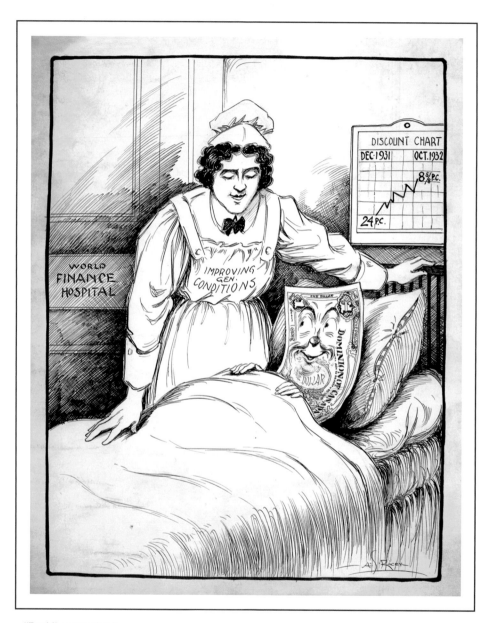

"Rapidly recovering."
Editorial cartoon by Arthur Racey, *Montreal Star*, October 1932

notes in circulation by reducing their gold backing to 25 per cent did not have much impact on the Canadian dollar. In the economic circumstances of the time, and given similar developments in the United States, this move was viewed as appropriate and elicited little market reaction (Bryce 1986, 143). The Canadian dollar returned to rough parity with its U.S. counterpart by 1934 (Chart 3) and, at times, even traded at a small premium. With the U.S. dollar depreciating against gold and the pound sterling, the Canadian dollar returned to its old parity with sterling.

Establishment of a central bank

Not surprisingly, as the 1930s progressed with little sign that the Depression was ending, pressure began to mount on the government to do something. In addition to concerns about the adequacy of the Finance Act, there was also widespread public distrust of the banking system, largely because of the high cost and low availability of credit. Farmers, especially those in western Canada, who were suffering from a sharp fall in both crop yields and prices, were particularly critical of banks and consequently very supportive of the formation of a central bank. They hoped that a central bank would be a source of steady and cheap credit. With effective nominal interest rates on farm loans in excess of 7 per cent, real interest rates were very high—about 17 per cent in 1931 and 1932, owing to sharply declining consumer prices. But interest rates were high for everyone because of the high Advance Rate. The traditional rate for a prime commercial loan was 6 per cent, while the standard deposit rate was 3 per cent, until the latter was reduced to 2.5 per cent in 1933 with the approval of the federal government (MacIntosh 1991, 73–75).

In July 1933, the government set up a commission with a mandate to study the functioning of the Finance Act and to make "a careful consideration of the advisability of establishing in Canada a Central Banking Institution . . . ." (Macmillan Report 1933, 5).[66] Lord Macmillan, a famous British jurist and known supporter of a central bank, was chosen by Prime Minister Bennett to chair the commission. The other members were Sir Charles Addis, a former director of the Bank of England; Sir William T. White, the former wartime Canadian Finance Minister and banker; John Brownlee, Premier of Alberta; and Beaudry Leman, a Montréal banker.[67]

---

66. Bordo and Redish (1986) argue that the establishment of the Bank of Canada had more to do with political than with economic imperatives. Watts (1993, 9), citing a 7 December 1933 speech by Prime Minister Bennett in London, Ontario, argues that the rationale for establishing a central bank was largely external. In the speech, Bennett stated that for Canada to be "financially independent," it needed a central bank for "determining balances, or settling international accounts." See also MacIntosh (1991).

67. From 1929 to 1931, Lord Macmillan had chaired a British commission called the Committee on Finance and Industry, which examined banking, finance, and credit developments in the United Kingdom. Sir Charles Addis was Chairman of the Hong Kong and Shanghai Banking Corporation and former Vice-Chairman of the Bank for International Settlements. Sir William White was Vice-Chairman of the Canadian Bank of Commerce. Mr. Beaudry Leman was General Manager of the Banque Canadienne Nationale and former president of the Canadian Bankers Association (Stokes 1939).

Public hearings began on 8 August 1933, and the final report was presented to the government less than seven weeks later on 28 September. While the commission voted only narrowly in favour of the establishment of a central bank, its conclusion was never really in doubt. The two British members of the committee, joined by Brownlee, voted in favour of a central bank, a position supported by both the Conservative government and the Liberal opposition.

The Canadian bankers on the committee opposed. White dissented from the majority on the grounds that it was unwise to establish a central bank in the prevailing uncertain economic environment. In his view, a newly established and untried central bank might hinder the government. Favouring a return to the gold standard, White contended that Canada's main problem was excessive debt (Macmillan Report 1933, 89). Leman shared this view and also believed that the establishment of a central bank raised constitutional issues that needed exploring (Macmillan Report 1933, 95).

In general, Canadian banks opposed the formation of a central bank. Reasons cited included concerns about the availability of central banking expertise in Canada, the absence of a Canadian money market, the ineffectiveness of the Federal Reserve in countering the Depression in the United States, and the long-time stability of the Canadian banking system. Banks were also unanimously concerned about a reduction in their

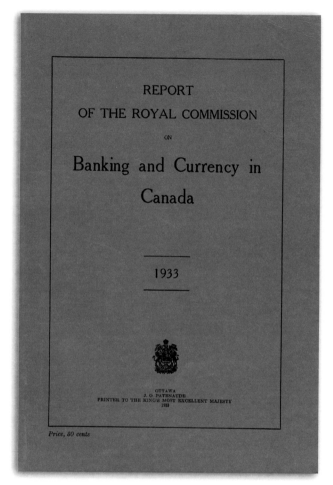

REPORT
OF THE ROYAL COMMISSION
ON

Banking and Currency in
Canada

1933

OTTAWA
J. O. PATENAUDE
PRINTER TO THE KING'S MOST EXCELLENT MAJESTY
1933

Price, 50 cents

Macmillan Report, cover, 1933
The Macmillan Report is a seminal document in the history of the Bank of Canada. It records the recommendations of the Royal Commission, chaired by Lord Macmillan, that considered the feasibility of establishing a central bank in Canada.

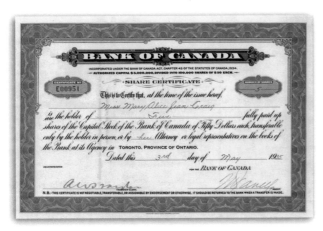

Bank of Canada, share certificate, 1935
The Bank of Canada was established as a widely held, privately owned institution, and shares with a par value of $50 were sold to the general public on 17 September 1934; $12.50 payable on application, with the balance due on 2 January 1935. Following a change of government, the Bank was fully nationalized by 1938.

Bank of Canada, $5, 1935 series
These notes were part of the first series issued by the new central bank. It was the only series to feature separate English and French notes. A portrait of Edward, Prince of Wales, appears on the left and the official seal of the Bank of Canada is on the right.

profits associated with the loss of their note-issuing privileges (MacIntosh 1991, 76).

The Bank of Canada Act received royal assent on 3 July 1934, and the central bank officially started operations on 11 March 1935.[68] Graham Towers, who had been assistant general manager of the Royal Bank, became the central bank's first Governor. To provide some practical central banking experience, J. A. C. Osborne, former secretary of the Bank of England, was made deputy governor.

The Dominion Notes Act and the Finance Act were also repealed on 11 March. Dominion notes were quickly replaced by new Bank of Canada notes. A revised Bank Act governing the operations of the chartered banks also took effect in 1934. Revisions to this act initiated a gradual phase-out of private bank notes in favour of Bank of Canada notes.

With the conduct of monetary policy now in the hands of the Bank of Canada, a dedicated monetary institution, there were greater prospects for a more activist monetary policy. However, the

---

68. The Bank of Canada, like most central banks of the time, was initially privately owned. Bank of Canada shares had to be widely held; no individual could own more than 50 shares. In 1936, following a Liberal victory in the election of 1935, Mackenzie King's government took control of the Bank through the acquisition of a second issue of shares and subsequently nationalized it in 1938.

BANK OF CANADA
STATEMENT OF ASSETS AND LIABILITIES
as at 31st December, 1935

LIABILITIES			ASSETS		
CAPITAL:			RESERVE—at market values:		
Authorized	$ 5,000,000.00		Gold Coin and Bullion	$180,509,342.65	
Issued and Paid Up		$ 5,000,000.00	Silver Bullion	1,638,365.96	
REST FUND		173,092.16	Sterling Funds	219,235.47	
NOTES IN CIRCULATION		99,677,228.95	U.S.A. Funds	4,003,866.07	
DEPOSITS:			Funds of other Countries on a Gold Standard	9,215.29	$186,380,025.44
Dominion Government	$ 18,262,843.88		SUBSIDIARY COIN		128,777.87
Chartered Banks	181,636,033.98		ADVANCES TO DOMINION GOVERNMENT		3,465,812.50
Other Banks	766,255.05	200,665,132.91	INVESTMENTS—at not exceeding market values:		
DIVIDEND DECLARED—payable 2nd January, 1936		113,000.00	Dominion Government short-term Securities	$ 30,873,168.86	
OTHER LIABILITIES		2,026,697.84	Other Dominion Government Securities	83,409,675.57	114,282,844.43
			BANK PREMISES (Furnishings and Equipment) at cost less amounts written off		111,911.25
			OTHER ASSETS		3,285,780.37
		$307,655,151.86			$307,655,151.86

G. F. TOWERS,
Governor.

J. A. C. OSBORNE,
Deputy Governor.

H. R. EXTENCE,
Chief Accountant.

PROFIT AND LOSS ACCOUNT
31st December, 1935

Profits from 11th March, 1935, to 31st December, 1935, after making provision for Contingencies and Reserves		$764,228.31
Appropriated as follows:		
Dividend No. 1 payable 2nd July, 1935, @ 4½% per annum on $12.50 from 21st September, 1934, to 2nd January, 1935, and on $50.00 from 2nd January, 1935, to 30th June, 1935	$126,000.00	
Dividend No. 2 payable 2nd January, 1936, @ 4½% per annum on $50.00 from 1st July, 1935, to 31st December, 1935	113,000.00	
	239,000.00	
Contribution to the Civil Service Superannuation and Retirement Funds	5,951.82	244,951.82
Balance		$519,276.49
Transferred to Rest Fund	$173,092.16	
For credit to Receiver General of Canada—account Consolidated Revenue Fund	346,184.33	
		$519,276.49

AUDITORS' REPORT TO SHAREHOLDERS

We have examined the above Statement of Assets and Liabilities of the Bank of Canada as at 31st December, 1935, and report that, in our opinion, it is properly drawn up so as to exhibit a true and correct view of the state of the Bank's affairs as at that date, according to the best of our information, the explanations given to us, and as shown by the books of the Bank. We have obtained all the information and explanations we have required.

G. T. CLARKSON, F.C.A.,
of the firm of Clarkson, Gordon, Dilworth & Nash.

J. A. LaRUE, C.A.,
of the firm of LaRue & Trudel.

Auditors

OTTAWA, 15th January, 1936.

Bank of Canada balance sheet
The Bank of Canada's first balance sheet, 31 December 1935

Bank maintained the Bank Rate (which was equivalent to the Advance Rate under the Finance Act) at the same 2.50 per cent rate that it had inherited. It was not until February 1943, in the midst of the war, that the Bank Rate was cut (Chart C2 in Appendix C).

Another important piece of legislation was the Exchange Fund Act, which received royal assent on 5 July 1935. The primary purpose of the act was to provide a fund that could be used to "aid in the control and protection of the external value of the Canadian monetary unit" (*Statutes of Canada* 1935). The resources of the Exchange Fund came from the profits associated with the revaluation of the Bank of Canada's gold holdings from the old statutory price of Can$20.67 per ounce to the prevailing world market price of US$35 per ounce.[69] Although the Exchange Fund Act was passed in 1935, the section of the act dealing with the use of the fund to protect the value of the Canadian dollar was not put into effect until 15 September 1939, following Canada's entry into World War II.

In any event, an Exchange Fund Account was not required to stabilize the Canadian dollar during the mid-1930s. With the currency trading in a relatively narrow range around parity with its U.S. counterpart, little intervention by the Bank of Canada was required.

By late 1938, as the international political climate deteriorated, the Canadian dollar began to slip, falling to a small discount of roughly 1 per cent against the U.S. dollar. The decline was modest, however, compared with that of the pound sterling, which fell by roughly 6 per cent in the second half of 1938, reflecting a considerable shift of funds out of the United Kingdom (Bank of Canada *Annual Report 1939*, 13).

After several months of relative stability, the Canadian dollar came under renewed, and this time significant, pressure in the last days of August 1939, as world tensions increased and funds moved to the safety of the United States. The Canadian dollar fell roughly 6 per cent vis-à-vis the U.S. dollar in the two weeks prior to Canada's declaration of war with Germany on 10 September 1939, and by another 3 per cent by the time the government imposed foreign exchange controls in mid-September (Bank of Canada *Annual Report 1940*, 12). The pound sterling fell even more sharply, declining from US$4.86 to US$4.06, a depreciation of roughly 14 per cent, before the imposition of exchange controls in the United Kingdom in early September.

---

69. Under the Bank of Canada Act, the government transferred to the Bank of Canada the gold that had backed the old Dominion notes. The gold holdings of the chartered banks that were held against Canadian-dollar liabilities were also transferred to the Bank of Canada. Revaluation proceeds amounted to $73.5 million, of which $10.5 million was returned to the chartered banks and $63 million credited to the Exchange Fund Account (Watts 1993, 23).

Laying the cornerstone for the Bank of Canada, 10 August 1937
Prime Minister Mackenzie King (left) and the Bank's first Governor, Graham Towers (right) watch as the stone is lowered into place.

Canada under Fixed Exchange Rates and Exchange Controls (1939–50)

Bank of Canada, $2, 1937
The 1937 issue differed considerably in design from its 1935 counterpart. The portrait of King George VI appeared in the centre of all but two denominations. The colour of the $2 note in this issue was changed to terra cotta from blue to avoid confusion with the green $1 notes. This was the Bank's first issue to include French and English text on the same note.

The war years (1939-45)

Exchange controls were introduced in Canada through an Order-in-Council passed on 15 September 1939 and took effect the following day, under the authority of the War Measures Act.[70] The Foreign Exchange Control Order established a legal framework for the control of foreign exchange transactions, and the Foreign Exchange Control Board (FECB) began operations on 16 September.[71] The Exchange Fund Account was activated at the same time to hold Canada's gold and foreign exchange reserves. The Board was responsible to the minister of finance, and its chairman was the Governor of the Bank of Canada. Day-to-day operations of the FECB were carried out mainly by Bank of Canada staff.

The Foreign Exchange Control Order authorized the FECB to fix, subject to ministerial approval, the exchange rate of the Canadian dollar vis-à-vis the U.S. dollar and the pound sterling. Accordingly, the FECB fixed the Canadian-dollar value of the U.S. dollar at Can$1.10 (US$0.9091)

---

70. Parliament did not, in fact, have an opportunity to vote on exchange controls until after the war. The Foreign Exchange Control Act received royal assent on 31 August 1946 and became effective on 1 January 1947. The legislation contained a "sunset" clause, which obliged the government to renew the controls every two years.

71. Preparations for the imposition of exchange controls in the event of war had begun in secret as early as August 1938. See Towers (1940).

Royal Bank of Canada, $5, 1943
In 1944, banks were prohibited from issuing their own notes. This note is from one of the last issues by a chartered bank. The Royal Bank's General Manager, Sydney G. Dobson, appears on the left, and President Morris W. Wilson on the right.

War savings stamps booklet, 1940
During World War II, citizens supported the war effort by buying war savings stamps at the post office and at banks. These stamps were glued into booklets and sent to the government for redemption in war savings certificates, which bore low interest and could be cashed in after the war.

buying and Can$1.11 (US$0.9009) selling. The pound sterling was fixed at Can$4.43 buying and Can$4.47 selling.[72] These rates were roughly consistent with market exchange rates immediately prior to the imposition of controls. Currency rates on futures contracts of up to 90 days were also fixed by the FECB. These exchange rates were maintained for the duration of the war.

To conserve Canada's foreign exchange and effectively support the value of the Canadian dollar, the Board introduced extensive controls. These controls allowed the Board to regulate both current and capital account transactions, although most current account transactions, other than travel, were treated fairly leniently.[73] Permits were required for all payments by residents to non-residents for imports of goods and services. Permits were also required for the purchase of foreign currencies and foreign securities, the export of funds by travellers, and to change one's status from resident to non-resident. Residents were also required to sell all foreign exchange receipts to an authorized dealer. Interbank trading in Canadian dollars ceased.

---

72. The spreads for both the U.S. dollar and the pound sterling were narrowed slightly in October 1945 by reducing the selling rate for the U.S. dollar to Can$1.1050 (US$0.9046) and Can$4.45 for the pound.
73. The Canadian government placed controls on the importation of goods deemed to be non-essential. Such import controls were administered by other bodies.

On 30 April 1940, the Foreign Exchange Acquisition Order stiffened the controls even further. Canadian residents, including the Bank of Canada, were now required to sell (with minor exceptions) all the foreign exchange they owned to the FECB.

The imposition of exchange controls by the Canadian authorities reflected a number of concerns (Handfield-Jones 1962). First, even though it was expected that Canadian exports to the United Kingdom would increase, there was a concern that the Canadian military buildup would lead to a significant rise in imports from the United States. Second, under U.S. law at the start of the war, loans to "belligerent" countries were forbidden. Hence, U.S. imports had to be paid for in cash; i.e., U.S. dollars or gold. Moreover, given British exchange controls, an increase in sterling assets arising from net Canadian exports to the sterling area could not be converted into U.S. dollars. Finally, there was a concern that Canadians might seek to place funds in a non-belligerent country and that U.S. residents, who held considerable Canadian assets, might seek to repatriate their holdings.

It is interesting to note that while all foreign currency transactions were subject to exchange controls, in practice, the controls centred on transactions involving U.S. dollars. Although permits were required for sterling transactions, there were no restrictions (FECB 1946, 19).

Moreover, Canadian residents were not required to sell sterling receipts to the FECB (Wonnacott 1958, 83). This reflected the buildup of sterling balances held by the FECB, which could not be converted into U.S. dollars.[74]

Canada's need for controls during World War II contrasts with its experience during World War I, when exchange controls were not imposed. In 1914, Canada's principal foreign creditor was the United Kingdom, with the bulk of British claims on Canada in the form of direct investment or denominated in sterling. British holdings of U.S. dollars were also substantial at the outbreak of World War I. Consequently, the British authorities were able to pay for their own U.S. imports, maintain a stable and convertible currency, and provide U.S. dollars to Canada in settlement of Canada's trade surplus with the United Kingdom.

The situation had changed by 1939. The United States had become Canada's most important source of foreign capital, and there was concern that neutral U.S. residents would not wish to hold the securities of a belligerent country. British holdings of U.S. dollars were also much diminished. Therefore, Canada could not expect the United Kingdom to provide U.S. dollars in exchange for surplus sterling balances, as it had in 1914. Indeed, the British authorities introduced their own exchange controls at the outbreak of World War II (FECB 1946, 9–10).

---

74. Efforts to reduce these sterling balances included interest-free loans to the United Kingdom and the repurchase of Government of Canada bonds issued in sterling, including those of the Canadian National Railway.

The revaluation of 1946

By late 1944, pressure on Canada's foreign exchange reserves had eased dramatically. The Hyde Park Agreement of April 1941, the entry of the United States into the war in December 1941, as well as major U.S. infrastructure projects on Canadian soil (such as the construction of the Alaska Highway) contributed to a rebuilding of Canada's foreign exchange reserves. There were also significant capital inflows into Canada, partly from Canadian residents repatriating funds invested in U.S. securities, but also from U.S. residents buying Canadian Victory Bonds. U.S. direct investment in Canada also increased.

The Hyde Park Agreement

The Hyde Park Agreement permitted Canada and the United States to specialize in the production of war material. Canada concentrated on the production of certain types of munitions, aluminum, and ships required by the United States (FECB 1946, 26). This agreement between Mackenzie King and Roosevelt was drafted, in longhand, by James Coyne, later to become Governor of the Bank of Canada, but who was then seconded to Clifford Clark, Deputy Minister of Finance, as Financial Attaché at the Canadian Embassy in Washington D.C.

The rebuilding of reserves allowed a slight easing of exchange controls in 1944 to facilitate travel to the United States and to allow Canadian firms to extend their foreign business activities. By the end of 1945, Canada's holdings of gold and U.S. dollars had increased to US$1,508 million from only US$187.6 million at the end of 1941.

With expectations of continued capital inflows, the Canadian dollar was revalued upwards by roughly 9 per cent against both the U.S. dollar and the pound sterling on 5 July 1946. The new rates were: Can$1.000 buying, Can$1.005 (US$0.9950), selling for the U.S. dollar; and Can$4.02 buying and Can$4.04 selling for the pound sterling. Interestingly, the rationale for the revaluation related more to dampening inflationary pressures emanating from the United States than to the buildup of reserves or to Canada's balance-of-payments situation. In a statement to the House of Commons, the minister of finance noted that the revaluation of the Canadian dollar was one of the measures taken to maintain order, stability, and independence in Canada's economic and financial affairs. He added that

> these measures we feel will go a long way toward insulating Canada against unfavourable external conditions and easing the inflationary pressures which are now so strong (Ilsley 1946, 3181).

"The new pilot."
Editorial cartoon by Jack Boothe, 9 July 1946. Reprinted with permission—*The Globe and Mail*

The devaluation of 1949

The new exchange rate did not hold for long. Imports from the United States rose sharply, leading to a marked decline in Canada's holdings of gold and U.S. dollars in the second half of 1946 and through 1947. While Canadian exports to the United Kingdom and other countries remained robust, they were financed largely by Canadian loans. Hence, they did not boost usable reserves.

In November 1947, Canadian authorities reduced travel allowances for Canadians visiting the United States and tightened import controls to restrict the importation of non-essential goods. The provision of U.S. dollars for Canadian direct investment abroad was also virtually suspended. Even with the intensification of exchange controls, Canada's holdings of gold and U.S. dollars declined to US$501.7 million by the end of 1947. These developments led to considerable criticism of the Canadian government for its 1946 decision to revalue the Canadian dollar.

The situation eased somewhat in 1948. Canada's trade deficit with the United States narrowed, a sizable U.S.-dollar line of credit was established with the U.S. Export-Import Bank, and Canada's trade balance with other countries improved (including an increase in actual receipts). In fact, by the end of 1948, Canada's holdings of gold and U.S. dollars had doubled to US$997.8 million.

Nevertheless, following a major realignment of the pound sterling and most other major European currencies vis-à-vis the U.S. dollar, the Canadian dollar was devalued by approximately 9.1 per cent against its U.S. counterpart on

"Free again."
Editorial cartoon, 2 October 1950. Reprinted with permission—
The Globe and Mail

20 September 1949.[75] The Canadian dollar thus returned to its pre-July 1946 value against the U.S. dollar of Can$1.10 (US$0.9091) buying and Can$1.105 (US$0.9050) selling. The FECB also established new official rates for the pound sterling: Can$3.0725 buying and Can$3.0875 selling.

The main reason cited for the Canadian dollar's devaluation was the possible effect of the substantial devaluations of other currencies on Canada's balance-of-payments position. There were also concerns that Canada's reserves had not recovered sufficiently from their 1947 low (FECB 1949, 7).

However, fast-changing international economic conditions, unleashed by the Korean War, placed the new fixed rate under pressure; this time on the upside. As a consequence, Canadian authorities were once again obliged to reconsider exchange rate policy, ultimately leading to the floating of the Canadian dollar in September 1950, and the lifting of exchange controls late the following year. These issues are explored in "A Floating Canadian Dollar," page 61.

The unofficial exchange market

Shortly after the imposition of exchange controls in 1939 and the official fixing of the Canadian dollar's value in terms of the U.S. dollar by the FECB, an unofficial market for Canadian dollars developed in New York that persisted until the Canadian dollar was floated at the end of September 1950. This was a legal market involving transactions in Canadian dollars between non-residents of Canada. Residents of Canada were prohibited from acquiring foreign exchange through the unofficial market. Similarly, no resident of

---

75. On 19 September 1949, the pound and the currencies of all other sterling-area countries, excluding Pakistan, were devalued by 30.5 per cent against the U.S. dollar. Concurrently, or shortly thereafter, the currencies of Sweden, Norway, Denmark, and the Netherlands were devalued by roughly 30 per cent. The currencies of other countries were devalued by smaller amounts—France by about 22 per cent, West Germany by 21 per cent, Portugal by 13 per cent, Belgium by 12 per cent, and Italy by 9 per cent.

Canada was ever authorized to convert foreign exchange into Canadian dollars through the unofficial market.

The source of "inconvertible" Canadian dollars consisted of Canadian-dollar bank balances held by non-residents when exchange controls were introduced in 1939, sales by U.S. residents of certain types of assets (such as real estate), and the proceeds of maturing Canadian-dollar securities paid to non-residents.

Canadian dollars purchased in the unofficial market could be used only in a very circumscribed manner. For example, they could not be used to purchase Canadian goods and services. In this regard, the purpose of exchange controls was not just to conserve available foreign exchange but also to maximize the receipt of foreign exchange. U.S. residents wishing to buy Canadian securities or real estate were, however, permitted to use Canadian dollars obtained in the unofficial market, as could travellers to Canada.

The unofficial market for Canadian dollars ended with the floating of the Canadian dollar. Throughout most of its existence, the inconvertible Canadian dollar traded at a sizable discount compared with its official counterpart (Chart 4). The spread between the two rates mirrored the pressures on the Canadian economy, widening to more than 10 per cent during the darkest months of 1940 and narrowing as the war progressed and Canadian prospects improved. By 1945, the

discount was temporarily eliminated. Indeed, for a few months during 1946, prior to the upward revaluation of the official Canadian dollar back to parity with its U.S. counterpart, the inconvertible Canadian dollar traded at a slight premium in the free market.

Chart 4
Canadian Dollar in Terms of the U.S. Dollar
Monthly averages (1939–50)

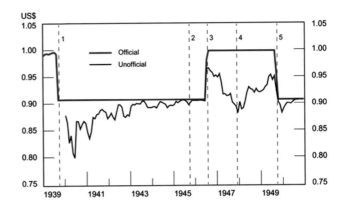

1. September 1939: War is declared, the Canadian dollar is fixed, and exchange controls are imposed.
2. September 1945: World War II ends.
3. July 1946: Canadian dollar revalued.
4. November 1947: Exchange controls tightened.
5. September 1949: Canadian dollar devalued.
Source: U.S. Board of Governors of the Federal Reserve System (1943, 1976)

Interestingly, when the official rate was finally revalued on 5 July 1946, the inconvertible Canadian dollar, while also appreciating, did not move up the whole amount. It generally traded between US$0.95 and US$0.96 through the remainder of that year. Clearly, the revaluation was not viewed as completely credible by free-market participants. Indeed, the free rate slowly weakened over the next few years, foreshadowing the eventual devaluation of the official rate in September 1949.[76]

The inconvertible Canadian dollar declined with the devaluation of the official exchange rate in 1949, but to a lesser extent, temporarily eliminating the differential between the two rates. With the inconvertible Canadian dollar continuing to weaken to about US$0.8840 through the winter of 1949–50, a differential of roughly 2.5 per cent temporarily re-emerged. The sudden improvement in Canada's economic prospects, however, and strong capital inflows from the United States, eliminated the differential between the two rates once again by March 1950. Indeed, the unofficial rate actually moved to a marginal premium to the official rate immediately prior to the decision to float the Canadian dollar.

The relevance of the unofficial rate

During the 1940s, there was an active debate over whether the unofficial rate was the "true" value of the Canadian dollar. The Bank of Canada maintained that, given the "limited use" of inconvertible Canadian dollars and the small size of the market, prices were not necessarily an accurate reflection of sentiment towards the Canadian dollar (FECB 1947, 5).[77]

This was disputed by many economists, including then-associate professor of economics, Milton Friedman. In a 1948 University of Chicago debate with Donald Gordon, Deputy Governor of the Bank of Canada, and Dr. W. A. Mackintosh, head of the economics department at Queen's University and wartime economic adviser to the government, Friedman argued that there was no particular reason why a small market should necessarily lead to a distorted price. He also argued strongly that Canada should introduce a flexible exchange rate rather than relying on a system of exchange controls to balance trade. Gordon, on the other hand, contended that a 10 per cent decline in the official Canadian dollar (to roughly the level prevailing in the unofficial market) would have comparatively little impact on trade flows (Friedman et al. 1948).

While there is no evidence directly linking Milton's Friedman's advice to Canada's subsequent decision to float the Canadian dollar, it undoubtedly had an impact on the internal thinking of the Bank of Canada.

---

76. The unofficial rate, after trading to a low of about US$0.9225 at the beginning of 1949, strengthened modestly to about US$0.9450 during the months immediately prior to the devaluation.

77. The Bank of Canada estimated that, on average, the unofficial market accounted for only 3 per cent of Canada's international transactions (Rasminsky 1946).

Poster for Canada Savings Bond campaign, ca. 1950

A Floating Canadian Dollar
(1950-62)

By mid-1950, the depreciation of the Canadian dollar against its U.S. counterpart the previous year, combined with rising commodity prices associated with the beginning of the Korean War in June 1950, had significantly strengthened Canada's trade balance with the United States. At the same time, the economic recovery in Europe, aided by the Marshall Plan, which provided European countries with convertible U.S. dollars, boosted Canadian exports (Muirhead 1999, 138). There were also strong inflows of direct investment into Canada. Short-term capital inflows also increased sharply, particularly through the third quarter of 1950, as speculation regarding a Canadian-dollar revaluation intensified.

In this environment, Canadian authorities became increasingly concerned about the inflationary impact of the inflows if Canada tried to maintain a fixed exchange rate. There was also concern that the inflows were leading to a "substantial and involuntary increase in Canada's gross foreign debt" (FECB 1950, 14).

On 30 September 1950, Douglas Abbott, the Minister of Finance, announced that

Today the Government, by Order in Council under the authority of the Foreign Exchange Control Act, cancelled the official rates of exchange which had been in effect since September 19th of last year . . . . It has been decided not to establish any new fixed parity for the Canadian dollar at this time, nor to prescribe any new official fixed rates of exchange. Instead, rates of exchange will be determined by conditions of supply and demand for foreign currencies in Canada.

He also announced that any remaining import prohibitions and quota restrictions, imposed in November 1947, would be eliminated, effective

2 January 1951. Controls on imports of capital goods were also to be reviewed.

Interestingly, the idea of floating the Canadian dollar was widely discussed as early as the beginning of 1949. A then-secret memorandum prepared in January of that year by James Coyne, then Deputy Governor of the Bank of Canada, made the case for floating the currency while retaining exchange controls. In his paper, Coyne noted that it would be better to "have a natural rate which could move up or down from time to time as economic conditions might require." He also noted that government inertia made it very difficult for the authorities to adjust a fixed exchange rate in a timely manner (Coyne 1949).

Options other than floating the exchange rate were apparently dismissed as impractical, including revaluing the Canadian dollar upwards, widening the currency's permitted ±1 per cent fluctuation band, or restricting capital inflows. Given the criticism levelled against the government after the 1946 revaluation of the Canadian dollar, followed by the short-lived 1949 devaluation, another revaluation was viewed as unacceptable. It was also unclear how much of a revaluation would be required to stem the capital inflows. Widening the bands also posed problems, since it was unclear how wide the bands would have to be. Likewise, restrictions on capital inflows were seen as untenable from a longer-term perspective for a country dependent on foreign capital (Hexner 1954, 248).

This view is consistent with a speech on exchange controls given by Douglas Abbott, Minister of Finance, in December 1951,

> The conclusion I have come to is that we would be better advised not to rely on exchange restrictions, but rather on the general handling of our domestic economic situation to keep us in reasonable balance with the outside world and to maintain the Canadian dollar over the years at an appropriate relationship with foreign currencies.

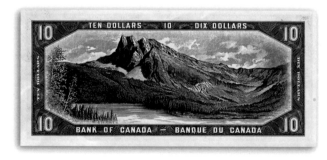

Bank of Canada, $10, 1954 series
This was the first note series to feature Canadian landscapes. These notes were simpler in design and more modern in style. This was also the only series to feature the reigning monarch on each denomination. This was popularly known as the "devil's head" series because of the image discernible in the Queen's hair.

The system envisaged by Coyne in 1949 of a floating Canadian dollar within a system of foreign exchange controls was put into practice when markets opened on 2 October 1950. With interbank trading now permitted, the Canadian dollar quickly appreciated, rising five cents to roughly US$0.95.

With the floating of the Canadian dollar, the rationale for the continuation of exchange controls came into question. Through 1951, controls were progressively eased. Finally, on 14 December 1951, the Foreign Exchange Control Regulations were revoked by an Order-in-Council. New regulations were passed that exempted all persons and all transactions from the need for permits to buy and sell foreign exchange. The Foreign Exchange Control Act itself, which had been renewed for another two-year period earlier in 1951, was repealed in October 1952.

After a quick rise to the US$0.95 level immediately after the float (Chart 5), the Canadian dollar continued to appreciate at a more gentle pace, moving to a small premium of about 2 per cent vis-à-vis the U.S. dollar by 1952. From then until the end of 1960, it traded in a relatively narrow range between US$1.02 and US$1.06. The peak for the Canadian dollar during this period was US$1.0614, touched on 20 August 1957. Foreign exchange intervention by the Bank of

Chart 5
Canadian Dollar in Terms of the U.S. Dollar
Monthly averages (1950–62)

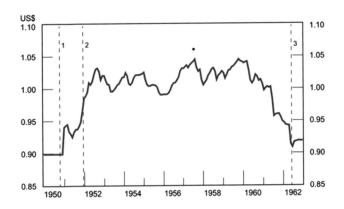

* 20 August 1957: Modern-day Canadian-dollar peak: US$1.0614
1. September 1950: Canadian dollar floated
2. December 1951: Exchange controls lifted
3. May 1962: Canadian dollar fixed
Source: Bank of Canada; U.S. Federal Reserve System (1976)

Canada through the Exchange Fund Account was limited to smoothing short-run fluctuations of the Canadian dollar.

While generally unpopular in business circles, the floating exchange rate was supported by many academic economists as a means of insulating the domestic economy from external shocks, either inflationary or deflationary.[78] It was also recognized

---

78. A fixed exchange rate required the Bank of Canada to direct monetary policy to maintaining the fixed rate. As a consequence, it could not pursue an independent monetary policy. Rather, it had to closely follow changes in U.S. interest rates, regardless of whether those interest rate changes were appropriate to Canadian circumstances. In contrast, a floating exchange rate gave the Bank of Canada the scope to direct policy at achieving and maintaining domestic price stability.

that the two-way risk associated with a flexible exchange rate could itself lessen large capital movements (Hexner 1954, 253).

Canada's successful experiment with a flexible exchange rate regime through much of the 1950s inspired considerable early academic work on the merits of a flexible exchange rate system. Later, it would provide a model for the rest of the world when the Bretton Woods system of fixed exchange rates finally collapsed during the early 1970s.

Conflict with the IMF

As a member of the International Monetary Fund (IMF), Canada's decision to float the Canadian dollar was at odds with its commitment to the Fund to maintain a fixed exchange rate within the Bretton Woods system. In this regard, in 1949 the Canadian authorities had established with the IMF a "par value" of US$0.9091 with a fluctuation band of ±1 per cent. The decision was also taken over the opposition of IMF staff who recommended more vigorous foreign exchange intervention or the imposition of controls on capital inflows (IMF 1950).[79] There were also concerns that Canada had "gravely compromised and embarrassed" the IMF and had set a bad example for other "less responsible members" (Goforth 1950).

"A 'profit' without honour in his own country."
Editorial cartoon by Les Callan, 1957

---

79. Given his close relationship with the IMF, the decision to float the Canadian dollar must have been difficult for Rasminsky. But since the economic argument in favour of a float was sound, he supported the decision. He also recognized that the international economic environment was not what had been expected. Unlike the 1930s, the predominant monetary issue of the day was inflation not deflation, and there had been no tendency towards competitive devaluations (Muirhead 1999, 140).

At least initially, floating was viewed as a temporary measure. The minister of finance noted the government's intention to remain in consultation with the Fund and

> ultimately to conform to the provisions of the Fund's Articles of Agreement which stipulate that member countries should not allow their exchange rates to fluctuate more than one percent on either side of the par values from time to time established with the Fund (Abbott 1950).

It would be almost 12 years before Canada reintroduced a fixed exchange rate and was again in the good graces of the IMF. Consequently, Canada came to be viewed as something of a maverick in international financial circles. The unwillingness to re-fix the exchange rate appears to have reflected concern about repeating the mistake of 1946 when the dollar was revalued upwards only to come under significant downward pressure the next year, followed by a devaluation in 1949. Subsequently, interest in re-pegging the currency waned as it seemed that Canada had the best of all worlds—a non-discriminatory trading system, an open capital market, and a reasonably stable exchange rate. While Canada's actions were not consistent with the IMF's practices, the outcome was certainly in line with its goals.

Establishment of the IMF

In July 1944, representatives from 44 countries met in Bretton Woods, New Hampshire to establish the post-war international financial architecture. Agreement was reached on creating the International Monetary Fund (IMF) which, among other things, would promote monetary co-operation and discourage competitive currency devaluations. After the IMF began operations in 1946, member countries agreed to establish "par values" for their currencies in relation to the U.S. dollar and to maintain them within narrow fluctuation bands. A par value change was permitted only to correct a fundamental disequilibrium. Louis Rasminsky, who was to become the Bank of Canada's third Governor, played a key role in the founding of the IMF, reconciling views and mediating between the British, led by John Maynard Keynes, and the Americans, led by Harry Dexter White. At Bretton Woods, Rasminsky chaired the key drafting committee (Muirhead 1999, 105). After the formation of the IMF, Rasminsky became Canada's first Executive Director, on a part-time, unpaid basis until September 1962, while remaining a senior official of the Bank of Canada (Muirhead 1999, 129).

Return to a Fixed Exchange Rate
(1962-70)

Canada, 92 ½ cents, Diefenbuck
"Political currency," so-called because it satirizes a politician or a political party and its policies, is private scrip that resembles a bank note but has no monetary value. The "Diefenbuck" was the result of the devaluation of the Canadian dollar against its U.S. counterpart during the 1960s that resulted from certain policies implemented under the administration of Prime Minister John Diefenbaker.

During the late 1950s, Canadian authorities became concerned about a deterioration in Canada's international competitiveness, aggravated by its strong dollar, which continued to be supported by substantial capital inflows. After the investment boom of the mid-1950s, economic activity had slowed significantly, and the unemployment rate more than doubled from 3.4 per cent in 1956 to 7.2 per cent in 1961. In this environment, the government sought to ease policy in order to support demand and reduce the economic slack in the economy.

James Coyne, who became Governor of the Bank of Canada on 1 January 1955, focused monetary policy on avoiding excessive domestic demand, keeping inflation in check, and reducing Canada's reliance on foreign savings. In favour of "sound" money, he was convinced that

> to engage in further large over-all monetary expansion in an attempt to drive down interest rates generally, with or without the motive of thereby reducing the inflow of capital from abroad, is an unsound and dangerous approach and would prove to be an ineffective approach, to the problems of the exchange rate, of the recession, and of achieving more consistent economic growth (Bank of Canada *Annual Report 1960*, 22).

Restrictive monetary policy at a time of relatively high unemployment and low inflation led to a sharp deterioration in relations between the

"Whee-e."

(James Coyne, Governor of the Bank of Canada, seated behind Donald
Fleming, Minister of Finance.)
Editorial cartoon, 30 December 1960. Copyright Duncan Macpherson.
Reprinted with permission—TorStar Syndication Services

Bank and the academic community.[80] In late 1960, twenty-nine prominent Canadian economists signed a letter calling for the dismissal of Governor Coyne.[81] At the same time, relations with the Diefenbaker government were also deteriorating. Determined to pursue an expansionary policy, the government did not believe that it had the support of the Governor.[82] The situation worsened when the government objected to the size of the Governor's pension, which had been agreed upon by the Bank's Board of Directors. The dispute, which became increasingly acrimonious and personal, came to a head on 30 May 1961, with the government requesting the resignation of Governor Coyne. The Governor refused. On 20 June, the minister of finance introduced an expansionary budget and announced that the government would take steps to lower the value of the Canadian dollar, including, as necessary, purchasing substantial amounts of U.S. dollars in the exchange market (Fleming 1961a). The government also introduced a bill in Parliament (An Act Respecting the Bank of Canada) to declare the position of Governor vacant (House of Commons 1961). The bill passed the House of Commons on 7 July, but after testimony by Governor Coyne, the Senate Standing Committee on Banking and Commerce concluded on 12 July that there had been no misconduct on

---

80. A 12 May 1962 article in *The Economist*, entitled "Inquest on a Floating Exchange Rate," opined that while a floating exchange rate arguably served Canada well in the period 1950–57, it was less clear thereafter because "domestic monetary policy itself began in these years to follow a perverse road." With interest rates remaining very high, the rate "ceased to behave in an anti-cyclical manner, and by its continuing buoyancy, did in fact exacerbate both the domestic problem of under-employment and the long-term problem of a yawning trade deficit."
81. See Gordon (1961).
82. The controversy over Coyne's policies provided the impetus for Robert Mundell's seminal work entitled, "The Appropriate Use of Monetary and Fiscal Policy for Internal and External Stability" (Mundell 1962).

his part. The following day, the full Senate confirmed the Committee's findings. Governor Coyne then resigned, viewing the decision of the Senate as a vindication of his conduct. Louis Rasminsky succeeded Coyne as Governor on 24 July 1961.[83]

Not surprisingly, the Canadian dollar began to weaken in this environment. From a level of about US$1.01 prior to the June budget statement, the dollar quickly fell to US$0.97. It weakened further in October 1961 to under US$0.96, following an announcement by the minister of finance that the appropriate discount of the Canadian dollar against the U.S. dollar "might well turn out to be greater than the present 3 per cent" (Fleming 1961b).

The introduction of a "managed" flexible exchange rate regime, under which the government would intervene to keep the Canadian dollar at a significant discount to its U.S. counterpart, as opposed to just smoothing fluctuations, was in some ways a compromise with the IMF. The Fund was encouraging Canadian authorities to return to a fixed exchange rate regime within the context of the Bretton Woods system. No new par value for the Canadian dollar was recommended, however. Additional time was seen as necessary to prepare for the re-establishment of a fixed rate.

After stabilizing at about US$0.95 between November 1961 and March 1962, the Canadian dollar began to weaken further, despite significant intervention by the Bank of Canada on behalf of the government to support the currency. On 2 May 1962, the government, in agreement with the IMF, established a new par value for the Canadian dollar, fixing it at US$0.9250 with a fluctuation band of ±1 per cent.

A press statement released by the Office of the Minister of Finance, Donald Fleming, stated that although a floating exchange rate had its advantages

> the Government has concluded that it would be desirable to give those engaged in international transactions firm assurance of stability with regard to the exchange rate . . . . The new rate of 92½ has been established after careful assessment of all the factors involved including the attitudes in the foreign exchange market and the nature of the exchange transactions which have been taking place in recent months.[84]

Fixing the exchange rate at a markedly lower level did not, however, relieve the pressure on the Canadian dollar. Doubts remained about the viability of the new rate, particularly given the prevailing political uncertainty.[85] Heavy official intervention was therefore required to hold the Canadian dollar within its allowed fluctuation band.

---

83. See Bélanger (1970) for a review of events.

84. It has been reported that Fleming wanted assurances that the dollar would not drop below US$0.90 if it were to float freely. Naturally, officials could not give this assurance, despite their belief that an equilibrium rate was well above that level. The US$0.9250 rate at which the Canadian dollar was fixed was apparently chosen by virtue of it being halfway between US$0.95 and US$0.90 (Helliwell 2005–06).

85. On 18 June 1962, a minority Conservative government was elected.

On 24 June 1962, the government announced a major economic and financial program aimed at restoring confidence in the Canadian dollar and indicated its determination to defend the currency's new par value. Measures taken included a tightening of fiscal and monetary policy, the imposition of temporary import surcharges, and the marshalling of US$1,050 million in financial support from the international community. This support consisted of a US$300 million drawing from the IMF,[86] a US$400 million line of credit from the U.S. Export-Import Bank, US$250 million under a reciprocal swap facility between the Bank of Canada and the Federal Reserve Bank of New York, and US$100 million from the Bank of England under a similar arrangement.[87] Other European central banks were also willing to provide additional assistance, if necessary (Bank of Canada *Annual Report 1962*, 8).

This program restored confidence in the Canadian dollar. The resumption of private capital inflows during the second half of 1962 enabled the Canadian authorities to gradually ease the emergency measures imposed earlier. Much of the international financial assistance received, excluding that of the IMF, was repaid by the end of the year. Funds owed to the IMF were fully repaid by 1964. For the remainder of the decade, the Canadian dollar was maintained, relatively easily for the most part, within

"**Broken kite.**"
Editorial cartoon, 9 May 1962. Copyright Duncan Macpherson. Reprinted with permission—TorStar Syndication Services

the permitted fluctuation band of ±1 per cent around its US$0.9250 par value.

The dollar did, however, come under significant, temporary downward pressure during the summer of 1963, following the U.S. announcement

---

86. A large proportion of the resources drawn from the IMF represented the liquidation of Canada's "reserve position in the Fund," which forms part of Canada's international reserves. Actual use of Fund credit amounted to US$138 million.

87. Through 1962, the Federal Reserve System entered into a series of reciprocal facilities with the central banks of most industrialized countries aimed at providing mutual short-term financial assistance. The arrangement with the Bank of Canada was originally for US$250 million. Over time, it increased and currently stands at US$2 billion. While most of these reciprocal facilities have been discontinued, the facility with the Bank of Canada is renewed annually.

on 18 July that it would impose an "Interest Equalization Tax" on foreign borrowings in U.S. capital markets.[88] Although Canada's current account deficit had narrowed significantly over the previous two years, it was still large. Consequently, there was a general fear that unless Canadian interest rates rose by an offsetting amount (roughly 1 percentage point per year), capital inflows from the United States would cease. On 31 July, the United States agreed to exempt Canada from the tax, with the proviso that Canada would not increase its foreign international reserves through the proceeds of borrowing in the United States (Bank of Canada *Annual Report 1963*, 6). Downward pressure on the currency ceased with this agreement, and Canadian markets stabilized.

The Canadian dollar experienced another bout of temporary downward pressure in March 1968, after the U.S. announcement of controls on capital outflows. The pressure eased with an agreement on 7 March that exempted Canada from all such controls. Similar to the exemption from the Interest Equalization Tax, Canada agreed that the U.S. balance-of-payments position would not be impaired as a result of its actions.

Because of concerns about the Bank of Canada's ability to conduct monetary policy in light of these accords, there was a follow-up agreement with the United States on 17 December 1968, which

Bank of Canada, $1 commemorative note, 1967
To commemorate Canada's centennial, the Bank of Canada issued $1 notes modelled on the 1954 issue but including special features such as the stylized maple leaf and the dates 1867–1967. This was the second and, to date, last commemorative note issued by the Bank.

stated that no particular level of reserves would have to be targeted (Bank of Canada *Annual Report 1968*, 13). This made it easier for the Bank to intervene in foreign exchange markets during periods of upward pressure on the currency.[89]

---

88. The objective of the Interest Equalization Tax was to restrain capital outflows from the United States. As Canada was a large borrower in the New York market, it was feared that capital flows to Canada would be reduced unless Canadian borrowers were exempted from the tax.
89. The U.S. Interest Equalization Tax, as well as the capital controls, were eliminated on 29 January 1974.

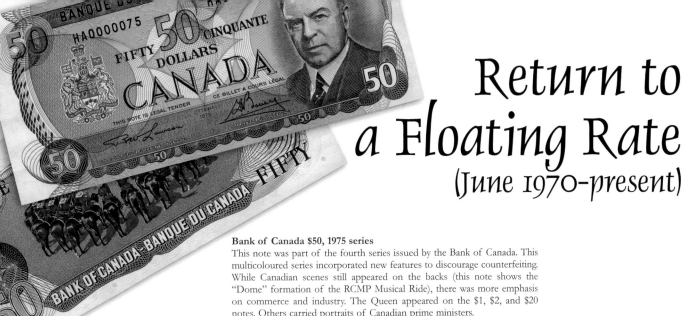

Return to a Floating Rate
(June 1970-present)

Bank of Canada $50, 1975 series
This note was part of the fourth series issued by the Bank of Canada. This multicoloured series incorporated new features to discourage counterfeiting. While Canadian scenes still appeared on the backs (this note shows the "Dome" formation of the RCMP Musical Ride), there was more emphasis on commerce and industry. The Queen appeared on the $1, $2, and $20 notes. Others carried portraits of Canadian prime ministers.

Rising domestic inflation led to the establishment of the Prices and Incomes Commission in 1968 and to the introduction of a restrictive stance on monetary policy. This occurred at a time when the United States was pursuing expansionary policies associated with the Vietnam War and with a major domestic program of social spending. Higher commodity prices and strong external demand for Canadian exports of raw materials and automobiles led to a sharp swing in Canada's current account balance, from a sizable deficit in 1969 to a large surplus. Combined with sizable capital inflows associated with relatively more attractive Canadian interest rates, this put upward pressure on the Canadian dollar and on Canada's international reserves. The resulting inflow of foreign exchange led to concerns that the government's anti-inflationary stance might be compromised unless action was taken to adjust the value of the Canadian dollar upwards.[90] There was also concern that rising foreign exchange reserves would lead to expectations of a currency revaluation, thereby encouraging speculative short-term inflows into Canada.

On 31 May 1970, Finance Minister Edgar Benson announced that

for the time being, the Canadian Exchange Fund will cease purchasing sufficient U.S. dollars to keep the exchange rate of the Canadian dollar in the market from exceeding its par value of 92½ U.S. cents by more than one per cent (Department of Finance 1970).

---

90. Consumer prices were rising at about 4 to 5 per cent through 1969 and early 1970. Wage settlements were also rising, touching 9.1 per cent during the first quarter of 1970.

"Look Ma, no thumb."
Editorial cartoon by James Reidford, 2 June 1970. Reprinted with permission—*The Globe and Mail*

Canadian authorities also informed the IMF of their decision to float the Canadian dollar and of their intention to resume the fulfillment of their obligations to the Fund as soon as circumstances permitted. The Bank of Canada concurrently lowered the Bank Rate from 7.5 per cent to 7 per cent, an action aimed at making foreign borrowing less attractive to Canadian residents and at moderating the inflow of capital, which had been supporting the dollar.

The government made the decision to float the Canadian dollar reluctantly. But Benson believed that there was little choice if the government was to bring inflation under control. He hoped to restore a fixed exchange rate as soon as possible but was concerned about a premature peg at a rate that could not be defended.

As in 1950, other options were considered but rejected. A defence of the existing par value was untenable since it could require massive foreign exchange intervention, which would be difficult to finance without risking a monetary expansion that would exacerbate existing inflationary pressures. A new higher par value was rejected, since it might invite further upward speculative pressure, being seen by market participants as a first step rather than a once-and-for-all change. Widening the fluctuation band around the existing fixed rate from 2 per cent to 5 per cent was rejected for the same reason (Beattie 1969). The authorities also considered asking the United States to reconsider Canada's exemption from the U.S. Interest Equalization Tax. Application of the tax to Canadian residents would have raised the cost of foreign borrowing and, hence, would have dampened capital inflows. This, too, was rejected, however, because of concerns that it would negatively affect borrowing in the United States by provincial governments (Lawson 1970a).

While recognizing the need for a significant appreciation of the Canadian dollar, the Bank of Canada saw merit in establishing a new par value at US$0.95 with a wider fluctuation band of ±2 per cent (Lawson 1970b). A new fix was seen as being more internationally acceptable than a temporary float, and since the lower intervention limit of about US$0.9325 would have been the same as the prevailing upper intervention limit, such a peg would have been accepted by academics who favoured a crawling peg. A new peg was also viewed as desirable because it would preserve an explicit government commitment to the exchange rate consistent with its obligations to the IMF. There was also some concern that a floating exchange rate might "encourage, as it had in the late 1950s, an unsatisfactory mix of financial policies" (Lawson 1970a).

For its part, the IMF urged Canada to establish a new par value. Fund management was concerned about the vagueness of Canada's commitment to return to a fixed exchange rate, fearing that the float would become permanent as it had during the 1950s. The IMF also feared that Canada's action would increase uncertainty within the international financial system and would have broader negative repercussions for the Bretton Woods system, which was already under considerable pressure. Canadian authorities declined to set a new fix, emphasizing the importance of retaining adequate control of domestic demand for the continuing fight against inflation.

The dollar in the 1970s

Immediately following the government's announcement that it would allow the Canadian dollar to float, the currency appreciated sharply, rising roughly 5 per cent to about US$0.97. It continued to drift upwards through the autumn of 1970 and into 1971 to trade in a relatively narrow range between US$0.98 and US$0.99. By 1972, the Canadian dollar had traded through parity with its U.S. counterpart. It reached a high of US$1.0443 on 25 April 1974.

The strength of the Canadian dollar through this period can largely be attributed to strong global demand, which boosted the prices of raw materials. There were also large inflows of foreign capital, partly reflecting the view that Canada's balance of payments was expected to be less affected by the tripling of oil prices that occurred through 1973 than that of other major industrial countries, since it was only a small net importer of oil.

During the early 1970s, the dollar's strength was also due to the general weakness of the U.S. currency against all major currencies as the Bretton Woods system of fixed exchange rates collapsed. With the U.S. balance-of-payments deficit widening to unprecedented levels, the U.S. government suspended the U.S. dollar's convertibility into gold on 15 August 1971 and imposed a 10 per cent surcharge on eligible imports. This action followed a series of revaluations of major currencies. On 18 December 1971, the major industrial countries agreed (the Smithsonian Agreement) to a new pattern of parities for the major currencies (excluding the Canadian dollar) with a fluctuation band of ±2.25 per cent. The U.S. dollar was also devalued by 8.57 per cent against gold, although it remained inconvertible. This last-ditch attempt to save the Bretton Woods system failed. By 1973, all major currencies were floating against the U.S. dollar.

The strength of the Canadian dollar against its U.S. counterpart during this period concerned the authorities, who feared the impact of a higher dollar on Canada's export industries at a time of relatively high unemployment. Various measures to rectify the problem were examined but dismissed as being either unworkable or harmful. These included the introduction of a dual exchange rate system, the use of moral suasion on the banks to limit the run-down of their foreign currency assets, and government control of the sale of new issues of Canadian securities to non-residents. None of these options was ever pursued (Government of Canada 1972). However, under the Winnipeg Agreement, reached on 12 June 1972, chartered banks agreed, with the concurrence of the minister of finance, to an interest rate ceiling on large, short-term (less than one year) deposits. The purpose of the agreement was to reduce "the process of escalation of Canadian short-term interest rates" (Bank of Canada *Annual Report 1972*, 15). Lower Canadian short-term interest rates and narrower rate differentials with the United States helped to relieve some of the upward pressure on the Canadian dollar.

Introduction of monetary targets

In reaction to "stagflation," the combination of high unemployment and inflation that prevailed during the early 1970s, most major economies, including Canada, embraced "monetarism." Based on work by Milton Friedman, who argued that inflation was always and everywhere a monetary phenomenon, it was maintained that by targeting a gradual deceleration in the growth of money, inflation could be brought under control with minimal cost. Accordingly, in 1975, the Bank of Canada adopted a target for the growth of M1, a narrow monetary aggregate, which it hoped, if met, would gradually squeeze inflation out of the system. Money growth would subsequently be set at a rate that would be consistent with the real needs of the economy, but would also ensure price stability over the long run. While appealing in theory, monetarism failed in practice. Despite the Bank of Canada hitting its money-growth targets, inflation failed to slow as expected. Monetary targets were abandoned in Canada in 1982. See page 77 for more details.

Monetary policy was also more accommodative than it should have been through this period, as the Bank of Canada sought to moderate the upward pressure on the currency and to support aggregate demand as the global economy slowed because of the oil-price shock. In hindsight, the Bank failed to "recognize the extent to which the economy in general and the labour market in particular were coming under strain" (Bank of Canada *Annual Report 1980*, 17). In other words, the Canadian economy was operating closer to its capacity limits than was earlier believed. Fiscal policy was also very expansionary through this period. While the 1974–75 slowdown in Canada was relatively shallow compared with that in the United States, where policy was less accommodative, inflationary pressures intensified.

To address these inflationary pressures, an anti-inflation program, including wage and price controls, was introduced by the government in late 1975, and the Bank of Canada adopted a target for the narrow monetary aggregate, M1, with the objective of gradually reducing the pace of money growth and thus inflation. After weakening temporarily in 1975 and falling below parity with the U.S. dollar, the Canadian dollar recovered in 1976. Wide interest rate differentials with the United States provided considerable support for the currency, with provinces, municipalities, and Canadian corporations borrowing extensively in foreign capital markets. Foreign appetite for Canadian issues was enhanced by the removal in 1975 of the 15 per cent federal non-resident

Canada, $1, Trudeau just-a-buck, 1972
This example of "political currency" satirizes former Prime Minister Pierre Trudeau and was circulated during the campaign of 1972 prior to his second term in office.

withholding tax on corporate bonds of five years and over. Foreign borrowing helped to mask the effects of deteriorating Canadian economic fundamentals on the Canadian dollar.

The currency moved up to the US$1.03 level during the summer of 1976 in volatile trading, but the election of a Parti Québécois government in Quebec on 15 November 1976 prompted markets to make a major reassessment of the Canadian dollar's prospects. Political uncertainty, combined with softening prices for non-energy commodities, concerns about Canada's external competitiveness related to rising cost and wage pressures, and a substantial current account deficit, sparked a protracted sell-off of the dollar.

Over the next two years, the Canadian dollar fell significantly, declining to under US$0.84 by the end of 1978. This occurred even though the U.S. dollar was itself depreciating against other major overseas currencies and despite considerable exchange market intervention by the Bank of Canada on behalf of the federal government to support the Canadian dollar. To help replenish its international reserves, the federal government established a US$1.5 billion stand-by line of credit with Canadian banks in October 1977. This facility was increased to US$2.5 billion the following April. A similar US$3 billion facility was organized in June 1978 with a consortium of U.S. banks. The federal government also borrowed extensively in New York and in the German capital market to assist in financing the current account deficit and to support the currency. The Bank of Canada tightened monetary policy through 1978, with the Bank Rate rising by 375 basis points to 11.25 per cent by the beginning of January 1979. Early in 1979, the federal government undertook additional foreign borrowings, this time in the Swiss and Japanese capital markets.

Notwithstanding the tightening in monetary policy, inflation pressures did not abate, even though the rate of monetary expansion was kept in line with announced targets, and the Bank Rate touched 14 per cent by the end of 1979. Against this backdrop, however, the Canadian dollar steadied and ended the year close to US$0.86.

Editorial cartoon, 19 June 1979. Copyright Duncan Macpherson. Reprinted with permission—TorStar Syndication Services

The dollar in the 1980s

Throughout the 1980s, the Canadian dollar traded in a wide range, weakening sharply during the first half of the decade, before staging a strong recovery during the second half. Early in the period, the Bank's policy was to moderate the effects of large swings in U.S. interest rates on Canada, taking some of the impact on interest rates and some on the exchange rate (Bank of Canada *Annual Report 1980*). For the Bank to react in this way, it needed more flexibility, and in March 1980, the Bank Rate was linked to the rate for three-month treasury bills, which was established at the weekly bill auction.[91] Canadian short-term interest rates rose sharply through 1980 and into the summer of 1981, with the Bank Rate touching an all-time high of 21.24 per cent in early August 1981, before moderating through the remainder of the year. At the same time, the Canadian dollar came under significant downward pressure. Important factors behind its depreciation included political concerns in the lead up to the Quebec referendum in May 1980, weakening prices for non-energy commodities, and the introduction of the National Energy Program by the federal government in October 1980, which prompted a wave of takeovers of foreign-owned firms by Canadian-owned firms, particularly in the oil sector. By mid-1981, policy-makers became concerned that the exchange rate slide would begin to feed on itself. Consequently, the minister of finance asked the chartered banks to reduce their lending to finance corporate takeovers that would involve outflows of capital from Canada.

Nevertheless, confidence in the Canadian dollar continued to erode through 1982 on concerns about the commitment of Canadian authorities to an anti-inflationary policy stance, and the cancellation of a number of large energy projects. With the dollar falling below US$0.77, the Bank of Canada allowed short-term interest rates to rise to prevent the increasing weakness of the Canadian dollar "from turning into a speculative rout" (Bank of Canada *Annual Report 1982*, 20). The Bank also reluctantly announced in November 1982 that it would no longer target M1 in its fight against inflation. Among other things, financial innovation had undermined the link between money growth and inflation. Research also revealed that the small changes in interest rates needed to keep money growth on track were insufficient to really affect prices or output. In testimony before the House of Commons Finance Committee, Governor Bouey said "We did not abandon M1, M1 abandoned us" (House of Commons 1983, 12). In other words, narrow money growth had failed to provide a reliable monetary anchor.

While the currency recovered to about US$0.82 on the Bank of Canada's actions and on positive market reaction to the introduction of a restrictive budget by the federal government, the respite proved to be short-lived. Although for the most part, the Canadian dollar held its own against its U.S. counterpart through 1983, it weakened sharply in 1984 and the first half of 1985, as did other major currencies, as funds were attracted to the United States by high interest rates and relatively favourable investment opportunities.

In September 1985, amid growing concerns about global external imbalances and speculative pressures in favour of the U.S. dollar, the G-5 major industrial countries agreed in the Plaza Accord to bring about an orderly depreciation of the U.S. dollar through a combination of more forceful concerted exchange rate intervention and domestic

---

91. The Bank Rate had previously been set in this manner between late 1956 and early 1962.

The Plaza and Louvre Accords

Named after the Plaza Hotel in New York, the Plaza Accord was a 1985 agreement among France, West Germany, Japan, the United States, and the United Kingdom aimed at correcting large external imbalances among major industrial countries and resisting protectionism. In addition to encouraging an orderly depreciation of the U.S. dollar, each country agreed to specific policy measures that would boost domestic demand in countries with a surplus, notably Japan and West Germany, and increase savings in countries with deficits, especially the United States. Two years later in Paris, the G-5 countries, along with Canada, agreed to intensify their economic policy coordination in order to promote more balanced global growth and to reduce existing imbalances. It was also agreed that currencies were now broadly in line with economic fundamentals and that further exchange rate shifts would be resisted. The success of policy coordination among industrial countries remains a hotly debated issue. While global protectionist pressures were averted, overly expansionary policy in Japan contributed to a speculative bubble in asset prices that subsequently collapsed, causing considerable and lasting damage to the Japanese economy. The ability of concerted exchange rate intervention to influence the value of the U.S. dollar has also been the subject of considerable controversy.

Editorial cartoon by John Collins, *Montreal Gazette*, 1986

policy measures. Although the overseas currencies began to appreciate against the U.S. dollar, the Canadian dollar continued to depreciate against its U.S. counterpart on concerns about weakening economic and financial prospects in Canada and falling commodity prices. The failure of two small Canadian banks—the Canadian Commercial Bank and the Northland Bank—may have also temporarily weighed against the Canadian dollar.

After touching a then-record low of US$0.6913 on 4 February 1986, the dollar rebounded, following a concerted strategy of aggressive intervention in the foreign exchange market, sharply higher interest rates, and the announcement of large foreign borrowings by the federal government. Initially stabilizing at about US$0.72, the dollar began an upward trend against the U.S. dollar, which lasted through the remainder of the decade.

In February 1987, Canada joined other major industrial countries in the Louvre Accord aimed at intensifying policy coordination among the major industrial countries and stabilizing exchange rates. Pursuant to this Accord, Canada participated on several occasions in joint interventions to support the U.S. dollar against the German mark and the Japanese yen. Although the Canadian dollar dipped briefly following the stock market "crash" in October—the Toronto Stock Exchange (TSE) fell 17 per cent over a two-day period—it quickly recovered.

Through 1988 and 1989, the currency continued to strengthen owing to various factors, including a buoyant economy led by a rebound in commodity prices, expansionary fiscal policy at both the federal and provincial levels, and a significant tightening of monetary policy aimed at cooling an overheating economy and reducing inflationary pressures. Positive investor reaction to the signing of the Free Trade Agreement (FTA) with the United States in 1988 also supported the currency.[92] The Canadian dollar closed the decade at US$0.8632.

The dollar in the 1990s

While the Canadian dollar began the 1990s on a strong note, it weakened against its U.S. counterpart through much of the decade, declining from a high of US$0.8934 on 4 November 1991 to close the decade at US$0.6929.

Through 1990 and most of 1991, the Canadian dollar climbed against its U.S. counterpart (and against major overseas currencies). This was largely due to a further tightening of monetary policy within the context of inflation-reduction targets announced in February 1991, and widening interest rate differentials that favoured Canadian instruments.

After cresting in the autumn of 1991 at its highest level against the U.S. dollar since the late 1970s, the Canadian dollar began to depreciate, falling sharply through 1992 to close the year at US$0.7868. The gradual, but sustained decline in the value of the Canadian dollar, which continued through 1993 and 1994, reflected various factors. With inflation falling to—and for a time below—the target range established in 1991 and with significant unused capacity in the economy, the Bank of Canada sought easier monetary conditions through lower interest rates. Downward pressure on the currency also reflected increasing concern about persistent budgetary problems at both the federal and provincial levels, softening commodity prices, and large current account deficits.

---

92. The appreciation of the Canadian dollar following the signing of the FTA gave rise to a myth at that time that the Canadian government had secretly agreed to engineer a higher value for the Canadian dollar as a quid pro quo for the free trade agreement with the United States.

Editorial cartoon by Brian Gable, 11 January 1995. Reprinted with permission—*The Globe and Mail*

The international environment was also unfavourable. The Exchange Rate Mechanism in Europe came under repeated attack through 1992 and 1993, followed by rising U.S. interest rates through 1994. The Mexican peso crisis of 1994 and early 1995 also drew investor attention to the weakness of Canada's fundamentals, especially its large fiscal and current account deficits.

A degree of stability in the Canadian dollar was temporarily re-established through 1995 and 1996 for a number of reasons. These included higher short-term interest rates (at least early in the period), evidence that fiscal problems were being resolved, a marked improvement in Canada's balance of payments, partly because of strengthening commodity prices, and a diminished focus on constitutional issues. The Canadian dollar traded in a relatively narrow range close to US$0.73 through much of this period.

Introduction of inflation targets

In February 1991, the government and the Bank of Canada set out a path for inflation reduction, with the objective of gradually lowering inflation, as measured by the consumer price index (CPI), to 2 per cent, the midpoint of a 1 to 3 per cent target range, by the end of 1995. An explicit commitment to an inflation target provided a nominal anchor for policy, helped to shape market expectations about future inflation, and improved central bank accountability. The target range of 1 to 3 per cent was subsequently extended on three occasions to the end of 2006. With much of the short-run movement in the CPI caused by transitory fluctuations in the prices of a few volatile components (e.g., gasoline), the Bank focuses, for operational purposes, on a measure of core CPI inflation that excludes eight of the most volatile components of the CPI and adjusts the rest to remove the impact of changes in indirect taxes.

Renewed weakness in the currency began to emerge in 1997 and became increasingly apparent in 1998, despite strong domestic fundamentals— very low inflation, moderate economic growth, and solid government finances. Once again, the slide of the currency could be partly attributed to external factors in the form of lower commodity prices. Commodity prices began to soften in the summer of 1997 but subsequently weakened significantly, owing to a financial and economic crisis in emerging markets in Asia. In this regard, the weaker Canadian dollar acted as a shock absorber and helped to mitigate the impact of lower commodity prices on aggregate demand and activity in Canada.

The large negative interest rate differentials that had earlier opened up between Canadian and U.S. financial instruments also weighed against the Canadian dollar, as did the U.S. dollar's role as a safe-haven currency during times of international crisis. Rising U.S. equity prices, reflecting a pickup in productivity growth and large capital flows into the high-technology sector, were another background factor that supported the U.S. currency against all others, including the Canadian dollar. This factor persisted though the rest of the decade.

During the summer of 1998, the crisis in emerging-market economies widened and intensified with a debt default by Russia and growing concerns about a number of Latin American countries. The Canadian dollar touched a low of US$0.6311 on 27 August 1998, before recovering somewhat following aggressive action by the Bank of Canada, including a 1 percentage point increase in short-term interest rates and considerable intervention in the foreign exchange market. While a lower Canadian dollar was not surprising, given the weakness in global commodity prices, the authorities had become concerned about increased

Exchange market intervention

The Bank of Canada last intervened in the foreign exchange market on behalf of the government on 27 August 1998. Up to this point, Canada's policy had been to intervene systematically to resist, in an automatic fashion, significant upward or downward pressure on the Canadian dollar. In September 1998, the policy was changed as intervention to resist movements in the exchange rate caused by fundamental factors was ineffective. Neither the government nor the Bank of Canada target a particular level for the currency, believing that the value of the Canadian dollar is best set by the market. Over time, the value of the Canadian dollar is determined by economic fundamentals. Canada's current policy is to intervene in a discretionary manner in foreign exchange markets only on the most exceptional basis, such as periods of market breakdown, or extreme currency volatility. For more information, see the Bank of Canada's website at www.bankofcanada.ca.

risk premiums on Canadian-dollar assets and a potential loss of confidence on the part of holders of Canadian-dollar financial instruments. Interest rate reductions by the Federal Reserve Bank and the return of a modicum of stability in financial markets following action by the Federal Reserve to calm markets after the collapse of Long-Term Capital Management (LTCM), permitted the Bank of Canada to reduce Canadian interest rates without undermining confidence in the Canadian dollar.[93]

The final year of the decade saw the Canadian dollar recouping some of its earlier losses against the U.S. dollar as the international financial situation improved, and investors focused on Canada's strong economic fundamentals, including a narrowing current account deficit and strengthening global commodity prices.

Editorial cartoon, 26 February 2002, Bruce MacKinnon/artizans.com

The dollar in the 21st century

The Canadian dollar resumed its weakening trend in 2000 and 2001, and touched an all-time low of US$0.6179 on 21 January 2002. Through much of this period, the U.S. currency rose against all major currencies, reaching multi-year highs, supported by large private capital flows in the United States owing to continued robust U.S. growth and further strong productivity gains. A decline in commodity prices in 2001, caused by an abrupt slowdown of the global economy, led by the United States, also undermined the Canadian currency. In addition, markets were temporarily roiled by the terrorist attacks in the United States on 11 September.

In this economically and politically uncertain environment, central banks around the world lowered interest rates to support demand and provide liquidity to markets. The Bank of Canada reduced short-term interest rates by 375 basis points through 2001 and early 2002.

Through 2002, the Canadian dollar stabilized and then began to recover as the global economy picked up and as the U.S. dollar started to weaken against other currencies. It appreciated sharply through 2003 and 2004, peaking at over US$0.85 in November 2004, a level not seen for thirteen years. This was a trough-to-peak appreciation of roughly 38 per cent in only two years. The Canadian dollar's

---

93. LTCM was a well-respected hedge fund that included on its board two Nobel-Prize-winning economists, Myron Scholes and Robert Merton. It was highly leveraged, with assets of about US$130 billion on a capital base of about US$5 billion. The fund incurred large losses on trades in the swap, bond, and equity markets that occurred when market liquidity dried up and spreads between government bonds and other instruments unexpectedly widened sharply. LTCM also incurred losses on its portfolio of Russian and other emerging-market debt following the Russian default.

Bank of Canada, $20, 2004
The *Canadian Journey* series is the sixth note issue by the Bank of Canada. It features the same portraits and strong identifying colours that appeared on the previous series, but incorporates images that reflect Canadian values and achievements. The back of this note illustrates the theme of Canadian arts and culture with works by Canadian artist Bill Reid that feature Haida images.

Editorial cartoon, 5 May 2005, Bruce MacKinnon/artizans.com

rise reflected a robust global economy, led by the United States and emerging Asian markets (particularly China), which boosted the prices of Canada's commodity exports. As well, growing investor concerns about the widening U.S. current account deficit, undermined the U.S. unit against all major currencies. While the Canadian dollar settled back somewhat during the first half of 2005 as the U.S. dollar rallied modestly against all currencies, underpinned by rising U.S.-dollar interest rates, it began to strengthen again through the summer, supported by rising energy prices. Strengthening against all major currencies, the Canadian dollar touched a high of US$0.8630 on 30 September 2005. In late October, it was trading for the most part in a US$0.84–0.85 range, off its earlier highs as energy prices retreated.

Chart 6
Canadian Dollar in Terms of the U.S. Dollar
Monthly averages (1970–2005)

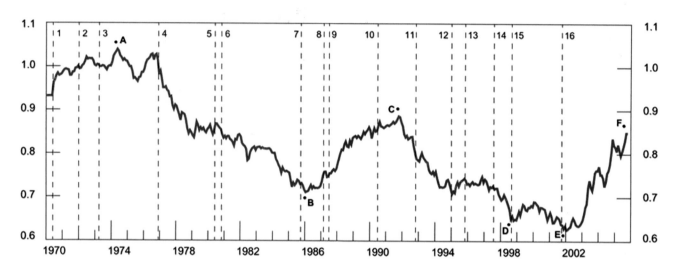

A: 25 April 1974: Canadian-dollar recent high US$1.0443
B: 4 February 1986: US$0.6913
C: 4 November 1991: US$0.8934
D: 27 August 1998: US$0.6311
E: 21 January 2002: All-time Canadian-dollar low US$0.6179
F: 30 September 2005: US$0.8630

Source: Bank of Canada

1. 31 May 1970: Canadian dollar floated
2. December 1971: Smithsonian Agreement
3. March 1973: Collapse of Bretton Woods system
4. 15 November 1976: Election of Parti Québécois in Quebec
5. 20 May 1980: Quebec Referendum
6. October 1980: National Energy Program introduced
7. September 1985: Plaza Accord
8. February 1987: Louvre Accord
9. 3 June 1987: Meach Lake Constitutional Accord
10. 26 June 1990: Ratification of Meach Lake Constitutional Accord fails
11. 26 October 1992: Defeat of Charlottetown Accord
12. December 1994: Mexican crisis begins.
13. 30 October 1995: Quebec Referendum
14. July 1997: Asian crisis begins.
15. 12 August 1998: Russian default crisis begins.
16. 11 September 2001: Terrorist attacks in the United States

Concluding Remarks

Canada's money provides a unique optic through which to examine this country's rich economic and political history. Through this lens, we can witness the clash of empires in the eighteenth century, the building of a continent-spanning nation during the nineteenth century, and the development of a "post-modern," bilingual, multicultural society in the late twentieth century.

We can also see the economic pressures brought to bear on Canada and the ingenuity of Canadians in dealing with them. Born of necessity, de Meulles' introduction of card money in 1685 is believed to be the first issue of paper money by a Western government. The Great Depression and deflation of the 1930s also challenged the orthodox monetary wisdom of the time, leading once again to monetary experimentation and to the creation of the Bank of Canada.

Canada's monetary history also illustrates the strong economic attraction of the United States, as well as the weakening economic and political ties with the United Kingdom. North-south economic linkages were the reason why Canada, over imperial opposition, chose the dollar instead of the pound as its monetary standard in the 1850s. However, in a typical Canadian compromise, both U.S. and British coins remained legal tender in Canada, alongside distinctive Canadian notes and coins, into the 1930s.

A similar tension can be found in Canada's choice of exchange rate regime. Through much of the nineteenth and early twentieth centuries, a fixed one-for-one exchange rate was maintained between Canada and the United States, supported by both countries' adherence to the gold standard. Such a relationship seemed natural in light of the close commercial and financial links between the two countries.

On the other hand, the Canadian economy, a major exporter of commodities, was, and remains, very different from that of the United States, a major supplier of manufactured goods. This distinction, as well as a desire in Canada to direct macroeconomic policy towards achieving domestic policy objectives, argues for a flexible exchange rate. These factors were the reasons why Canada adopted a floating exchange rate in 1950 and again in 1970.

Canada's history has shown, however, that no exchange rate regime is perfect. The choice of regime involves trade-offs that may change with the passage of time and with differing circumstances.

Dissatisfaction with the severe policy limitations of the gold standard led Canada and other countries to break the link between their currencies and gold during the 1930s. Dissatisfaction with the competitive devaluations and "beggar-thy-neighbour" policies of the Depression years led to the Bretton Woods system of fixed, but adjustable, exchange rates after the Second World War. Dissatisfaction with pegged exchange rates in an environment of global inflationary pressures and rising capital mobility led to the floating of all major currencies in 1973.

The launch of the euro on 1 January 1999 and the collapse of fixed exchange rate regimes in many emerging-market economies led to a renewed debate in Canada and abroad on appropriate exchange rate regimes. The debate in Canada was also fuelled by the persistent weakness of the Canadian dollar and a view held by some economists that a common North American currency was appropriate and, possibly, inevitable. But the weight of economic analysis and opinion continue to favour Canada maintaining its flexible exchange rate, and retaining its monetary policy independence.[94]

Until relatively recently, however, it was not clear that Canada and other countries with floating exchange rates had used their monetary independence to their best advantage. Immediately prior to the floating of the Canadian dollar in 1970, Harry Johnson, the great Canadian monetary economist, noted that

[a] flexible exchange rate is not, of course, a panacea; it simply provides an extra degree of freedom, by removing the balance-of-payments constraint on policy formulation (Johnson 1972).

This observation was prophetic. Through the following decades, exchange rates, liberated from the constraints imposed by the Bretton Woods system, moved in a wide range, reflecting both real and monetary shocks in the domestic economy and in the anchor country; i.e., the United States. The Canadian dollar was no exception. While countries were now free to direct policy at achieving domestic objectives, the "extra degree of freedom" was often squandered. In Canada, the rationale behind floating the Canadian dollar in 1970 was to avoid importing U.S. inflation. In the event, Canada's inflation performance was very similar to that of the United States. (See Chart A3 in Appendix A.)

David Laidler, a noted monetary economist and economic historian at the University of Western Ontario, has argued that a flexible exchange rate, unlike a fixed rate, is not a coherent monetary order, since a flexible rate does not "define a policy goal, but merely permits some other goal . . . to be pursued" (Laidler 2002). For a country with a flexible rate to have a coherent

---

94. For a review of the economic arguments for flexible exchange rates in North America, see Murray, Schembri, and St-Amant (2003). See also Murray and Powell (2003) for a discussion of the extent to which U.S. dollars are used in Canada. See also Thiessen (2000) and Dodge (2002).

monetary order, other elements are required—a clear goal for monetary policy (and a broader supportive policy framework that includes sustainable fiscal policy), credibility, and public accountability. Laidler contended that such a coherent monetary order was not firmly in place in Canada until about 1995. This was four years after inflation targets were introduced and 25 years after Canada last floated the dollar. It was only when a coherent monetary order was established that the Bank of Canada was in a position to use its policy independence to its best advantage by focusing on preserving the domestic purchasing power of the Canadian dollar through low inflation, while at the same time allowing the external value of the currency to adjust to shocks.

Appendix A
Purchasing Power of the Canadian Dollar

Inflation erodes the purchasing power of money. Even with a low annual inflation rate of 2 per cent (the midpoint of the Bank of Canada's 1 to 3 per cent target range for inflation since 1995), a dollar will lose half of its purchasing power in approximately 35 years. When the consumer price index (CPI) is used to measure inflation, the average annual rate of inflation in Canada since 1914 is 3.2 per cent. Thus, the Canadian dollar lost more than 94 per cent of its value between 1914 and 2005 (Chart A1). Alternatively, one dollar in 1914 would have the purchasing power of $17.75 in 2005 dollars.[1]

While consumer price data prior to 1914 are unavailable, a broader measure of inflation, the gross domestic product (GDP) deflator, is available back to 1870 (Leacy 1983). While the CPI and GDP deflator can diverge, they tend to move together over time. Since 1870, with annual GDP inflation averaging 3.6 per cent, the Canadian dollar has lost more than 96 per cent of its value. Again, this is equivalent to saying one Canadian dollar in 1870 would have the purchasing power of roughly $26.70 in today's money.

Chart A1
Purchasing Power of the Canadian Dollar
1914 = 100

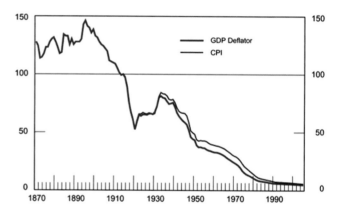

Source: Leacy (1983)

Periods of high inflation include the early years of the twentieth century, when major infrastructure projects in Canada were financed by large inflows of foreign capital, and the years during and immediately following the two world wars, owing to the cost of the war effort and

---

1. The Bank of Canada has an inflation calculator on its website (www.bankofcanada.ca) that shows changes in the costs of a fixed basket of consumer purchases from 1914 to the present.

Chart A2
Inflation in Canada
Year-over-year percentage change

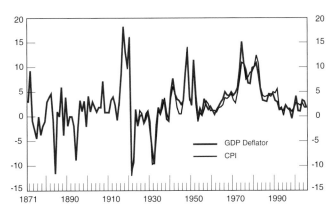

Source: Leacy (1983)

"The wearin' o' the green."
Editorial cartoon by Merle Tingley, ca. 1950–59

demobilization. More recently, high inflation was experienced during the 1970-80s, owing to the oil crises and policy errors (Chart A2).

In contrast, prices fell during the early 1920s, when Canada experienced deflation on its return to the gold standard and during the Great Depression of the 1930s. Prices also fell episodically during the last decades of the nineteenth century.

To provide a different perspective on the purchasing power of the Canadian dollar, Table A1

lists indicative prices of selected food staples since 1900. As can be seen, the cost of a pound of butter has risen from about 25 cents at the beginning of the twentieth century to about $4.00 today. At the same time, a labourer in 1901 would have earned 14 to 15 cents an hour in Halifax or Montréal and 23 cents in Toronto.[2] In contrast, the 2005

---

2.   Leacy (1983), "Hourly wage rates in selected building trades by city," series E248–267. The earliest available data point for a western province is 1906. At that time, the average labourer in Vancouver would earn 35 cents per hour.

Table A1
Indicative Prices of Selected Food Staples, December (dollars)

	1900	1914	1929	1933	1945	1955	1965	1975	1985*	1995	2005**
Beef (sirloin) per lb.	0.14	0.24	0.35	0.19	0.43	0.80	1.10	2.34	3.81	5.05	6.99
Bread (loaf)	0.04	0.05	0.08	0.06	0.07	0.13	0.18	0.43	1.00	1.30	1.79
Butter (one lb.)	0.26	0.35	0.48	0.26	0.40	0.64	0.63	1.11	2.51	2.87	4.01
Eggs (one dozen)	0.26	0.45	0.65	0.45	0.56	0.70	0.64	0.92	1.34	1.63	2.22
Milk (quart)	0.06	0.10	0.13	0.10	0.10	0.21	0.26	0.43	1.12	1.46	1.97

Source: The *Labour Gazette*, Dominion Bureau of Statistics, Statistics Canada
*October
**June

minimum wage in Canada ranged from $6.30 an hour in New Brunswick to $8.00 an hour in British Columbia.

In 1905, the average production worker in a factory earned $375 per year, while the average supervisory and office employee earned $846.[3] In 2004, the average annual income of a person working in the manufacturing sector was $42,713. The average manager's salary was $70,470.[4] A significant portion of the increase in salaries since the early 1900s would reflect the impact of inflation.

Other currencies also lost domestic purchasing power over time owing to inflation. In Chart A3, one can see that while Canada's accumulative inflation performance has been significantly better than that of the United Kingdom over the period since 1914, our performance has been largely the same as that of the United States. Only in the last ten years or so, has Canada averaged a lower rate of inflation than the United States.

In terms of gold, the Canadian dollar has depreciated markedly over the years, much of this occurring since the early 1970s. One ounce of gold was worth $20.67 in 1854 when the Currency Act was passed in the Province of Canada, fixing the Canadian dollar at par with the U.S.-dollar, equivalent to 23.22 grains of gold. In 1933, the statutory price of gold in Canada was the same, $20.67 per

---

3. Leacy (1983), "Annual earnings in manufacturing industries, production and other workers," series E41–48.
4. Statistics Canada, Manufacturing: Trades, Transport and Equipment Operators & Related Occupations and Manufacturing: Management Occupations.

ounce. The official U.S.-dollar price of gold was raised to US$35 per ounce (roughly the same in Canadian dollars) on 31 January 1934 when President Roosevelt's administration took steps to reflate the U.S. economy during the Great Depression. The US$35 per ounce price remained fixed until 15 August 1971 when President Nixon broke the link between the U.S. dollar and gold. In Canadian dollars, one ounce of gold was worth about $35.40 on that date. In late October 2005, the market price of an ounce of gold stood at roughly $550 in Canadian funds (or about US$465).[5] In other words, the Canadian dollar has lost about 96 per cent of its value in terms of gold since 1933, with much of this occurring since August 1971, while the U.S. dollar has lost roughly 95 per cent of its value.

Periods of rapid inflation, as well as episodes of significant deflation, in Canada over the past century or more underscore the importance of the Bank of Canada's objective of maintaining low, stable, and predictable inflation. If an economy is to perform well, its citizens must have confidence that the value of the money they use is broadly stable—that is to say subject to neither chronic inflation or deflation. Both inflation and deflation create uncertainty about the future and can have a significant negative impact on the economy. Their effects also do not fall equally on the population.

Chart A3
Consumer Price Index
(1914 = 100)

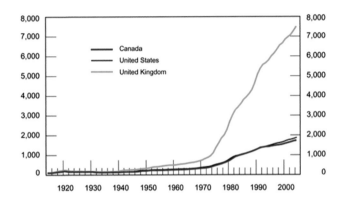

Source:
Canada - Statistics Canada
United States - Global Insight
United Kingdom - Office for National Statistics*
*Composite Price Index: 1913–47, Retail Price Index: 1948–2004

Unexpected inflation or deflation redistributes income and wealth, between borrowers and lenders, and between generations. Consequently, to avoid the burden that inflation or deflation imposes on an economy, it is important for a central bank to pursue a monetary policy that is firmly focused on achieving and maintaining price stability.[6]

---

5.   Since the price of gold was freed in 1971, it has moved in a wide range, trading as high as US$850.00 per ounce in January 1980.
6.   For more information on the benefits of price stability, see the May 1995 issue of the *Monetary Policy Report*, available on the Bank of Canada's website at www. bankofcanada.ca.

Appendix B
Alternative Money

This history has focused on legal tender money in Canada, that is to say money that has been approved by the authorities for paying debts or settling transactions. Canada also has a rich history of private money—coins and paper scrip produced by individuals and companies, which commanded sufficient confidence within a community that they circulated freely.

"Bons" and tokens

Through much of the colonial period in New France and later in British North America, merchants, and even individuals, issued paper scrip. The paper scrip was not backed by gold or silver but could be used to buy goods in the issuers' stores—a sort of IOU, which quickly began to change hands as money. The value of notes and the extent of their circulation depended on the reputation of the issuer.

In Upper and Lower Canada, such fractional notes (known as *bons* after "*Bon pour*," the French for "Good for," the first words on many such notes) circulated widely during the eighteenth and early nineteenth centuries. Fractional notes were also issued by merchants in the Atlantic

Montréal, George King note, 1772
This note and others issued by the local merchant George King were denominated in "coppers," a conventional designation for a halfpenny.

Halifax, merchant note, 5 shillings, 1820
Until the practice was outlawed in 1820, Halifax merchants commonly issued personalized scrip in low denominations to meet the need for coinage.

provinces. The widespread acceptance of *bons* (also called "shinplasters") helped to set the stage for the issuance of paper currency by commercial banks (Shortt 1986, 37).

Similar to "*bons*," brass and copper tokens circulated alongside legal tender coins and helped to offset a shortage of low-denomination coins, useful in small day-to-day transactions.[7] With a face value of a half a penny or penny, tokens were widely distributed by banks, non-financial companies, and individuals. While some tokens identified the issuer, many did not. Provincial governments also issued tokens. These so-called semi-regal tokens were not legal tender coins because they were not sanctioned by the authorities in London. Issuing tokens was a profitable business, since the cost of production was significantly lower than their denominated value.

While most early colonial tokens were taken out of circulation in the 1870s, when the new federal government reorganized Canada's copper coinage, trade tokens remained popular into the 1930s. Trade tokens were redeemable for goods and services of a given value (for example, a loaf of bread) and were issued by a wide range of companies. While these tokens were very successful in local communities, their popularity waned when transportation improved and business became less local in nature.

Bank of Montreal, halfpenny, 1839
The Bank of Montreal issued base-metal tokens for general circulation in the late 1830s and early 1840s. The rarest issue from this bank is the so-called "side views" that feature a view of the corner of the Bank of Montreal head office.

Merchant token, I. Carrière, ½ loaf, Buckingham, Quebec
From the late nineteenth through the mid-twentieth centuries, many Canadian businesses issued tokens as advertising and to encourage client loyalty. Typically made of brass or aluminum, they were redeemable by the issuer for the indicated item or service.

---

7.   Useful references include Breton (1894), Banning (1988), Cross (1990), and Berry (2002).

Today, Canadian Tire "money" represents the best-known modern equivalent of trade tokens. First introduced in 1958 as a "cash bonus coupon," Canadian Tire "money" constitutes a promotional reward program under which the scrip, which has no expiry date, is redeemable for goods at any Canadian Tire store in any amount. Canadian Tire "money" has sometimes been accepted by third parties in lieu of cash.

Canadian Tire coupon, 10 cents, 2002
Canadian Tire "money"—a Canadian icon

Prosperity certificates

During the Great Depression of the 1930s, a number of towns and cities issued scrip or certificates that circulated as money. In August 1936, Alberta's Social Credit Government, led by William Aberhart, issued "prosperity certificates."[8] These were issued in denominations of $1 and were used to pay relief workers on provincial public works projects. Additionally, the legislation allowed certificates to be put into circulation via special agreements with municipalities.

To promote the circulation of certificates, increase spending, and deter hoarding, holders were required to affix a one-cent stamp to the certificates every week to maintain their value. At the end of two years, the Government of Alberta promised to redeem the certificates using the proceeds of the stamp sales, with the residual (after paying the expenses related to the issuance of the certificates and the stamps) going to the government.

Prosperity certificates, quickly known as "funny money," were not well received by the general public who objected, among other things, to having to buy stamps to maintain their purchasing power. Most stores were also reluctant to accept them. Almost immediately, the Alberta Supreme Court issued an interim injunction halting a deal between the province and the city of Edmonton on the issuance and circulation of

---

8.   See *An Act Respecting Prosperity Certificates*, Alberta, 1936.

Alberta, $1, prosperity certificate, 1936

Community money

Communities, typically isolated ones such as islands, have sometimes issued scrip or alternative currencies that could be used locally to buy goods and services. In 1837, William Lyon Mackenzie issued dollar-denominated notes in the name of the Provisional Government of Upper Canada on Navy Island in the Niagara River, following his abortive attempt to seize Toronto in the Rebellion of 1837.

During the second half of the nineteenth century, private notes, denominated in dollars, were issued by Calvin & Son, a family-owned firm, on Garden Island, located in Lake Ontario near Kingston and then home to about 750 people. The company, which was principally involved in the timber and ship-building businesses, owned virtually everything on the island. Its notes could be used to buy goods in the company-owned general store (Swainson 1984).

Since 2001, Salt Spring Island, British Columbia, with a population of about 10,000, has issued its own alternative currency. Salt Spring Island dollars are issued by the Salt Spring Island Monetary Foundation, a not-for-profit society, whose objective is to maintain a local currency on

certificates by the city.[9] Following a subsequent decision by the government to redeem the certificates monthly instead of waiting two years, the stock of outstanding certificates declined sharply. The Alberta government finally abandoned the issuance of prosperity certificates in April 1937. At that time, only $12,000 were still in circulation out of $500,000 printed.[10]

9. The Court did not base this judgment on the constitutional merits of prosperity certificates, although it believed this to be a very important issue. Rather, the injunction reflected the fact that the payment of a stamp tax on the certificates by the city represented a burden on Edmonton tax payers and that the city did not have the authority to carry on business through two monetary systems, one based on legal tender, the other based on certificates. Although the Supreme Court of Canada apparently never gave an opinion on the prosperity certificates themselves, it ruled in 1938 that three pieces of Social Credit legislation (*An Act Respecting the Taxation of Banks, An Act to Amend and Consolidate the Credit of Alberta Regulations Act*, and *An Act to Ensure the Publication of Accurate News and Information*) were unconstitutional.

10. The Globe, 8 April 1937

Salt Spring Island, $$5, 2001
In 2001, the Salt Spring Island Monetary Foundation was established to issue note-like certificates to help fund community initiatives on this island off Canada's west coast. This note was designed by Warren Langley and Pat Walker.

convertibility, each Salt Spring Island dollar in circulation is backed by a reserve fund in the form of cash, term deposits, or gold. Certificates may be bought and redeemed on demand at participating stores, banks, and credit unions.

An interesting feature of Salt Spring Island dollars is that they are issued in limited editions. It is hoped that the attractive bills will be retained by visitors to the island as souvenirs. Net income generated by the reserve fund is used to help finance community projects.

the island for community projects and to promote local commerce and goodwill.[11]

The bills, which are considered to be gift certificates, are designed by local artists and are protected by sophisticated anti-counterfeiting devices. They are widely accepted by stores, individuals, and financial institutions on the island. While not legal tender, they are redeemable upon demand in Canadian currency. To ensure

---

11.   See www.saltspringdollars.com.

Appendix C
Charts

Chart C1
Canadian Dollar vis-à-vis U.S. Dollar and Pound Sterling
Annual average (1858–2005)

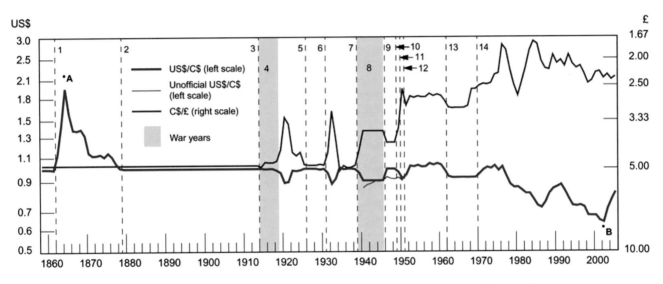

A: 11 July 1864: All-time Canadian-dollar high US$2.78
B: 21 January 2002: All-time Canadian-dollar low US$0.6179
1. January 1862: U.S. suspends convertibility.
2. January 1879: U.S. returns to gold standard.
3. August 1914: Canada suspends convertibility.
4. August 1914 to November 1918: World War I
5. July 1926: Canada returns to gold standard.
6. September 1931: U.K. abandons gold standard
   October 1931: Canada bans gold exports.

7. September 1939: Canada fixes dollar, introduces exchange controls.
8. September 1939 to September 1945: World War II
9. July 1946: Canada repegs dollar at parity.
10. September 1949: Canada devalues.
11. September 1950: Canada floats.
12. December 1951: Exchange controls end.
13. May 1962: Canada fixes.
14. May 1970: Canada floats.

Source: Bank of Canada; U.S. Federal Reserve System; *Historical Statistics of Canada* (Second Edition); Some Notes on Foreign Exchange in Canada before 1919 (S. Turk, June 27, 1962); *Montreal Gazette.*

Chart C2
Interest Rates: Canada, United Kingdom, and United States, 1914–2005

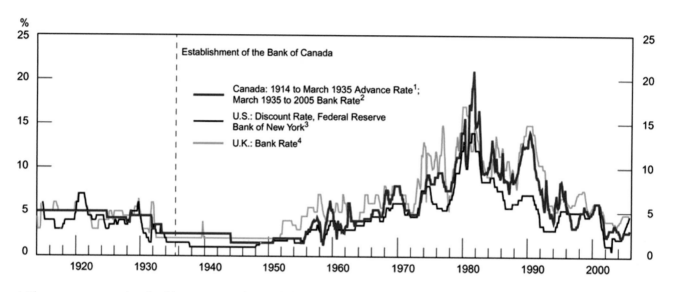

1. There were some exceptions. Special rates were sometimes applied to particular securities.
2. From 1 November 1956 to 24 June 1962 and from 13 March 1980 to 21 February 1996, the Bank Rate in Canada was ¼ of 1 per cent above the weekly average tender rate of 91-day treasury bills. Since 22 February 1996, the Bank Rate has been set at the upper limit of the Bank of Canada's operating band for the overnight interest rate.
3. Prior to January 2003, discount-window lending consisted of adjustment credit, extended credit, and seasonal lending programs. Customarily, the interest rate on adjustment credit was lower than the federal funds rate: the rate of interest at which banks lend to each other. After January 2003, the adjustment and extended credit programs were replaced by primary and secondary credit programs. Rates on primary and secondary credit are above the federal funds rate.
4. 1914 to June 1972 Bank Rate, 1972 to March 1981 Minimum Lending Rate, 1981 to October 1996 Min. Band 1 Dealing Rate 1, 1996 to present Repo Rate.

Source: U.S. Federal Reserve, Macmillan Report, Bank of Canada, Bank of England website

Bibliography

Abbott, D. 1950. Statement, 30 September.
_____. 1951. Debates, House of Commons, 14 December.

Anonymous. 1820. *An Enquiry into the Origin and Present System of Colonial Banks, and Their Dangerous Effects. With a Proposition for a National Bank.* Quebec: T. Cary, Jr. & Co.

Bank of Canada. *Annual Report.* Various issues.
_____. *Monetary Policy Report.* Various issues.
_____. 1990. *The Story of Canada's Currency.* 4th edition. Ottawa: Bank of Canada.

Banning, E.B. 1988. *Exploring Canadian Colonial Tokens.* Toronto: Charlton International Inc.

Beattie, J.R. 1969. "Memo Re: Widening of Exchange Rate Band." Bank of Canada memorandum, 10 April, Bank of Canada Archives LR06-522-230.

Beauchamp, W.M. 1901. "Wampum and Shell Articles Used by the New York Indians." *Bulletin of the New York State Museum* 41(8).

Beckhart, B.H. 1929. *The Banking System of Canada.* New York: Henry Holt and Company.

Bélanger, M. 1970. "The Coyne Affair: Analysis and Evaluation." MA thesis. University of Ottawa.

Berry. P. 2002. "Trade and Other Tokens of the Gatineau Region." *Up the Gatineau!* 28: 31–36. Chelsea, Que.: The Historical Society of the Gatineau

Binhammer, H.H. and P. Sephton. 1998. *Money, Banking and the Canadian Financial System.* 7th edition. Toronto: International Thomson Publishing.

Bordo, M. and F.E. Kydland. 1992. "The Gold Standard as a Rule." Federal Reserve Bank of Cleveland Working Paper No. 9205.

Bordo, M. and A. Redish. 1986. "Why Did the Bank of Canada Emerge in 1935?" NBER Working Paper No. 2079.
_____. 2005. "Seventy Years of Central Banking: The Bank of Canada in International Context, 1935-2005." NBER Working Paper No. 11586.

Brecher, I. 1957. *Monetary and Fiscal Thought and Policy in Canada, 1919–1939.* Toronto: University of Toronto Press.

Breckenridge, R.M. 1910. *The History of Banking in Canada.* National Monetary Commission, Washington: Government Printing Office.

Breton, P.N. 1894. "*Illustrated History of Coins and Tokens Relating to Canada.*" Montréal: P.N. Breton & Co.

Bryce, R.B. 1986. *Maturing in Hard Times: Canada's Department of Finance through the Great Depression.* Institute of Public Administration of Canada, McGill-Queen's University Press.

Canada. Department of Finance. 1970. News Release, 31 May.

Canada. Dominion Bureau of Statistics. *Prices and Price Indexes*. Various issues.

———. Statistics Canada. 1983. *Historical Statistics of Canada*, edited by F.H. Leacy. Ottawa: Supply and Services Canada.

———. Statistics Canada. *Consumer Prices and Price Indexes*. Various issues.

———. Statutes of Canada. 1935. 25-26 Geo. 5, c. 60.

———. Department of Labour. *The Labour Gazette*. Various issues.

Canadian Museum of Civilization. 2005. Website: <http://www.civilization.ca>.

Courchene, T.J. 1969. "An Analysis of the Canadian Money Supply: 1925–1934." *Journal of Political Economy* 77: 363–91.

Coyne, J.E. 1949. "A Method of Combining a Free Exchange Rate with the Present System of Exchange Controls in Canada." Bank of Canada memorandum, 31 January, Bank of Canada Archives GM89-1-3.

Creighton, J.H. 1933. *Central Banking in Canada*. Vancouver: Clarke & Stuart Co.

Cross, W.K. 1990. *The Charlton Standard Catalogue of Canadian Colonial Tokens*. 2nd edition. Toronto: The Charlton Press.

———. 2003. *The Charlton Standard Catalogue of Canadian Coins*. 57th edition. Toronto: The Charlton Press.

Davies, G. 2002. *A History of Money from Ancient Times to the Present*. 3rd edition. Cardiff: University of Wales Press.

Davis, R. 1867. *The Currency; What It Is and What It Should Be*. Ottawa: Hunter, Rose & Co.

Deutsch, J.J. 1940. "War Finance and the Canadian Economy, 1914–1920." *The Canadian Journal of Economics and Political Science* 6: 525–42.

Dick, T.J. and J.E. Floyd. 1992. *Canada and the Gold Standard: Balance-of-Payments Adjustment, 1871–1913*. Cambridge: Cambridge University Press.

Dimand, R. 2005. "David Hume on Canadian Paper Money: An Overlooked Contribution." *Journal of Money, Credit, and Banking* 37(4): 783–87.

Dodge, D. 2002. "Dollarization and North American Integration." Remarks to the Chambre de commerce du Québec, Sherbrooke, Quebec, 5 October.

The Economist. 1962. "Inquest on a Floating Exchange Rate." 12 May. 573–74.

Esler, G. 2003. "The Canadian Silver Nuisance, 1865-1870." *Chatter*. Chicago Coin Club. Website (May):<http://www.chicagocoin club.org/chatter/2003/>.

Fenton, P. 1993. "Historical Overview of the Canadian Exchange Rate." Bank of Canada memorandum, 1 December.

Fleming, D.M. 1961a. *Debates*, House of Commons, 20 June.

———. 1961b. Press Release, Office of the Minister of Finance (General), 27 October.

Flemming, H. 1921. *Halifax Currency*. Nova Scotia Historical Society.

Foreign Exchange Control Board (FECB). *Annual Report*. Various issues.

———. 1947. *Answers to Some Questions about the Unofficial Market in Canadian Dollars*.

Friedman, M., D. Gordon, and W.A. Mackintosh. 1948. "Canada and the Problems of World Trade." *Round Table*, 18 April. Chicago: University of Chicago.

Fullerton, D.H. 1986. *Graham Towers and His Times*. Toronto: McClelland and Stewart.

The Globe. 1936–37. Various issues.

Goforth, W. 1950. "Reactions to the New Canadian 'Floating' Rate." Bank of Canada memorandum, 18 October, Bank of Canada Archives Int. 4B-220 Vol. 1.

Gordon, H.S. 1961. *The Economists Versus the Bank of Canada*. Toronto: Ryerson Press.

Government of Alberta. 1936. *An Act Respecting Prosperity Certificates*.

Government of Canada. 1972. "The Problem of the Appreciation of the Canadian Dollar." Cabinet memorandum, 9 June, Bank of Canada Archives LR76-522-288.

Handfield-Jones, S.J. 1962. "Foreign Exchange Developments since the Formation of the Bank of Canada." Bank of Canada memorandum, 14 May, Bank of Canada Archives LR76-570-15-4.

Haxby, J.A. 1975. "Canada's Government Paper Money—Part 1." *Canadian Paper Money Journal* 11: 5–18.

Helleiner, E. 2003. *The Making of National Money: Territorial Currencies in Historical Perspective*. Ithaca: Cornell University Press.

Helliwell, J.F. 2005–06. "From Flapper to Bluestocking: What Happened to the Young Woman of Wellington Street?" *Bank of Canada Review* (winter) forthcoming.

Hexner, J.T. 1954. "The Canadian Exchange Rate." *Public Policy* 5: 233–68.

House of Commons. *Debates*. Various issues.

_____. 1983. "Minutes of Proceedings and Evidence." Standing Committee on Finance, Trade and Economic Affairs, No. 134, 28 March.

Ilsley, J.L. 1946. *Debates*, House of Commons, 5 July.

International Monetary Fund. 1950. "Executive Board Minutes." Executive Board Meeting 604, 30 September.

Johnson, H. 1972. *Further Essays in Monetary Economics*. London: George Allen & Unwin.

Journal of the House of Assembly, Lower Canada. 1830. 11 George IV, Appendix Q, 9 March.

Karklins, K. 1992. *Trade Ornament Usage among the Native Peoples of Canada: A Source Book*. Ottawa: Parks Service, Environment Canada.

Knox, F.A. 1939. "Dominion Monetary Policy, 1924–1934." A study prepared for the Royal Commission on Dominion-Provincial Relations. Ottawa.

_____. 1940. "Canadian War Finance and the Balance of Payments, 1914–18." *The Canadian Journal of Economics and Political Science* 6: 226–57.

Laidler, D. 2002. " Inflation Targets Versus International Monetary Integration: A Canadian Perspective." University of Western Ontario, EPRI Working Paper Series No. 2002-3.

Lainey, J.C. 2004. "La <*Monnaie des Sauvages*>; *Les Colliers de Wampum d'Hier à Aujourd'hui*." Sillery Québec: Septentrion.

Lawson, R.W. 1970a. "Exchange Rate Policy." Bank of Canada memorandum, 29 April, Bank of Canada Archives LR76-522-237.

_____. 1970b. "Notes on 95 +2." Bank of Canada memorandum, 21 May, Bank of Canada Archives LR76-522-241.

Leacy, F.H., editor. 1983. *Historical Statistics of Canada*. Second edition. Ottawa: Statistics Canada.

MacIntosh, R. 1991 *Different Drummers: Banking and Politics in Canada*. Toronto: Macmillan.

Macmillan Report. 1933. *Report of the Royal Commission on Banking and Currency in Canada*. Ottawa: J.O. Patenaude.

Martell, J.S. 1941. "A Documentary Study of Provincial Finance and Currency 1812–36." *Bulletin of the Public Archives of Nova Scotia, Halifax* II(4).

McArthur, D. 1914. "History of Public Finance, 1763–1840." In *Canada and its Provinces: A History of the Canadian People and their Institutions by One Hundred Associates*, edited by A. Shortt and A. Doughty, Vol. IV: 491–518. Toronto: Glasgow, Brook & Co.

McCullough, A.B. 1984. *Money and Exchange in Canada to 1900*. Toronto: Dundurn Press.

McQuade, R. 1976. "Halifax Currency in Nova Scotia." *Canadian Numismatic Journal* 21: 399–402.

The Montreal Gazette. 1864. Various issues.

Mossman, P.L. 2003. "Money of the 14th Colony: Nova Scotia (1711–1783)." *The Colonial Newsletter* 124: 2533–93. The American Numismatic Society.

Muirhead, B. 1999. *Against the Odds: The Public Life and Times of Louis Rasminsky*. Toronto: University of Toronto Press.

Mundell, R.A. 1962. "The Appropriate Use of Monetary and Fiscal Policy for Internal and External Stability." *International Monetary Fund Staff Papers* 9 (March): 70–76.

_____. 1998. "Uses and Abuses of Gresham's Law in the History of Money." Columbia University (August). Available at <http://www.columbia.edu/~ram15/grash.html>.

Murray, J. and J. Powell. 2003. "Dollarization in Canada: Where Does the Buck Stop?" *North American Journal of Economics and Finance* 14: 145–72.

Murray, J., L. Schembri, and P. St-Amant. 2003. "Revisiting the Case for Flexible Exchange Rates in North America." *North American Journal of Economics and Finance* 14: 207–40.

Pennington, J. 1848. *The Currency of the British Colonies*. London: W. Clowes.

Porter Commission. 1964. *Report*. Ottawa: Royal Commission on Banking and Finance.

Rasminsky, L. 1946(?). "Unofficial Market in Canadian Dollars." Bank of Canada memorandum, date unknown, Bank of Canada Archives INT2B-400.

Redish, A. 1984. "Why Was Specie Scarce in Colonial Economies? An Analysis of the Canadian Currency, 1796–1830." *Journal of Economic History* 44(3): 713–28.

Reid, R.L. 1926. *The Assay Office and the Proposed Mint at New Westminster*. Victoria: Charles F. Banfield Printer.

Rich, G. 1988. *The Cross of Gold: Money and the Canadian Business Cycle, 1867–1913*. Ottawa: Carleton University Press.

Roberts, P. 2000. "Benjamin Strong, the Federal Reserve, and the Limits to Interwar American Nationalism." Federal Reserve Bank of Richmond *Economic Quarterly* 86/2 (Spring): 61–98.

Rudin, R. 1985. *"Banking en français: The French Banks of Quebec, 1835–1925."* Toronto: University of Toronto Press.

Salt Spring Island Dollars. Website (October 2001): <http://www.saltspringdollars.com>.

Select Committee Appointed to Examine and Report on the Expediency of Establishing a Provincial Bank. 1835. *Report*. House of Assembly (Upper Canada), 13 February.

Shearer, R.A. and C. Clark. 1984. "Canada and the Interwar Gold Standard, 1920–35: Monetary Policy without a Central Bank." In *A Retrospective on the Classical Gold Standard, 1821–1931*, edited by M.D. Bordo and A.J. Schwartz, 277–310. NBER Conference Report. Chicago: University of Chicago Press.

Shortt, A. 1914a. "Currency and Banking, 1760–1841." In *Canada and its Provinces: A History of the Canadian People and their Institutions by One Hundred Associates*, edited by A. Shortt and A. Doughty, Vol. IV: 599–636. Toronto: Glasgow, Brook & Co.

Shortt, A. 1914b. "Currency and Banking, 1840–1867." In *Canada and its Provinces, A History of the Canadian People and their Institutions by One Hundred Associates*, edited by A. Shortt and A. Doughty, Vol. V: 261–91. Toronto: Glasgow, Brook & Co.

_____. 1925a. *Documents Relating to Canadian Currency, Exchange and Finance during the French Period*. Vol. I. Ottawa: F.A. Acland.

_____. 1925b. *Documents Relating to Canadian Currency, Exchange and Finance during the French Period*. Vol. II. Ottawa: F.A. Acland.

_____. 1933. *Documents Relating to Currency, Exchange and Finance in Nova Scotia with Prefatory Documents, 1675–1758*. Ottawa: J.O. Patenaude.

_____. 1986. *Adam Shortt's History of Canadian Currency and Banking, 1600–1880*. Reprinted by The Canadian Bankers' Association. Toronto: The Canadian Bankers' Association.

Stokes, M.L. 1939. *The Bank of Canada: The Development and Present Position of Central Banking in Canada*. Toronto: Macmillan Company.

Swainson, D. 1984. *Garden Island: A Shipping Empire*. Marine Museum of the Great Lakes at Kingston.

Thiessen, G. 2000. "Why a Floating Exchange Rate Regime Makes Sense for Canada." Remarks to the Chambre de commerce du Montréal métropolitain, Montréal, Quebec, 4 December.

Towers, G. 1940. "Sinews of War." An Address Presented at 'Study Course.' Foreign Exchange Review Board, 1 April.

Turk, S. 1962. "Some Notes on Foreign Exchange in Canada before 1919." Bank of Canada memorandum, 27 June, Bank of Canada Archives 4B-200, Vol 5.

Turley-Ewart, J. 1999. "Banking's Hidden Past." *Canadian Banker*, November/December.

Urquhart, M.C. 1986. "New Estimates of Gross National Product, Canada, 1870–1926: Some Implications for Canadian Development." In *Long-Term Factors in American Economic Growth*, NBER Studies in Income and Wealth, edited by S.L. Engerman and R.E. Gallman, Vol. 51: 9–94. Chicago: University of Chicago Press.

U.S. Board of Governors of the Federal Reserve System. 1943. *Banking and Monetary Statistics (1914–41)*. Washington.

_____. 1976. *Banking and Monetary Statistics (1941–70)*. Washington.

Vukson, W.B.Z. 2003. "Canadian Dollar Chaos: A Ten Year History." Toronto: (G7 Books).

Watts, G.S. 1993. *The Bank of Canada: Origins and Early History*. Ottawa: Carleton University Press.

Weir, W. 1903. *Sixty Years in Canada*. Montréal: John Lovell & Son.

Wikipedia. 2005. Website (October): <http://en.wikipedia.org/wiki/Main_Page>.

Willard, K.L., T.W. Guinnane, and H.S. Rosen. 1995. "Turning Points in the Civil War: Views from the Greenback Market." NBER Working Paper No. 5381.

Wonnacott, G.P. 1958. "The Canadian Dollar, 1948–1957." PhD dissertation, Princeton University.

Yeager, L.B. 1976. *International Monetary Relations: Theory, History, and Policy*. 2nd edition. New York: Harper & Row.

Young, G.R. 1838. *"Upon the History, Principles, and Prospects of the Bank of British North America, and of the Colonial Bank; with an Enquiry into Colonial Exchanges, and the Expediency of Introducing 'British Sterling and British Coin' in Preference to the 'Dollar,' as the Money of Account and Currency, of the North American Colonies."* London: Wm. S. Orr and Co.

Index

Note: "n" in a reference indicates a footnote;
"(i)" indicates an illustration.

Abbott, Douglas, 61, 62
Aboriginal money, *see* First Nations
Acquits, New France, 7
Act for Ascertaining the Rates of Foreign Coins in Her Majesty's Plantations in America (1707), 13n21
An Act Respecting the Bank of Canada (1961), 67
Addis, Sir Charles, 47, 47n67
Advance Rate
      deflationary effect (1920s), 44–45
      in early Depression years, 47
      during World War I, 38, 39, 40, 40n58
Alternative money, 92–96
Anti-counterfeiting devices, 17(i), 25(i)
Anti-inflation program, 75
Army bills (1812), 14(i), 15

Bank Act (1871), 28
Bank Act (1934), 49
Bank Circulation Redemption Fund, 28n47
Bank notes (issued by chartered banks)
      as backing for bank deposits, 37
      early 1800s, 17–19,
      no longer issued (1934), 49
      no longer legal tender (1926), 41
      security for, 28

      see also Bank of Canada notes; Government-issued notes
Bank of Canada, establishment (1934), 47–49, 49n68
Bank of Canada Act (1934), 49
Bank of Canada notes
      issues (1935 to 1969), 44(i), 49(i), 53(i), 62(i), 70(i), 71(i), 83(i)
      replacement for Dominion notes (1935), 49
Bank of Clifton (Zimmerman Bank), note, 25, 25(i)
Bank of Montreal
      halfpenny (1839), 93(i)
      notes, 16(i), 17, 25(i), 26(i), 28(i)
      tokens, 92(i)
Bank of New Brunswick, note, 18(i)
Bank of Nova Scotia, note, 17(i)
Bank of Upper Canada
      notes, 16(i), 26n40
Bank of Western Canada, 25
Bank Rate, 34, 51, 76
Banque Canadienne Nationale, note, 42(i)
Benson, Edgar, 71, 72
Bills of credit, 14–15
Bills of exchange, New France, 7n11, 8(i), 9
Bons (alternative money), 92
Boothe, Jack (editorial cartoon), 57(i)
Boston bills, 14

Bouey, Gerald, 77

Brass tokens, 92–93

Breckenridge, Roeliff, 25

Bretton Woods system (1944), 65, 74, 86

British colonial coinage, 11–20

British Columbia
    decimalization (1865), 24, 24n37
    Treasury notes, 16

British North America Act (1867), 26–27

Brownlee, John, 47, 48

Buchanan, Isaac, 23n34

Callan, Les (editorial cartoon), 64(i)

Canada, Province of, *see* Province of Canada

Canada Banking Company, 17n26

Canada Savings Bonds, 61(i)

Canadian Commercial Bank, 78

Canadian dollar
    in 1970s, 73–76
    in 1980s, 76–79
    in 1990s, 79–82
    in 21st century, 82–83
    during Depression, 45
    devaluation (1949), 57–58
    exchange rates, *see* Exchange rates
    under the gold standard (1854–1914), 33–36
    gold standard suspended (1914–26), 37–41
    gold standard, phasing-out (late 1920s), 41–43
    gold standard, return to (1926), 40
    "inconvertible" dollar (1939–50), 58–60
    notes, 39(i)
    official Canadian currency (1871), 27
    purchasing power of, 88–91
    revaluation (1946), 56
    unofficial exchange market (1939–50), 58–60
    see also Currency, Canadian

Canadian Journey series of bank notes (2004), 83(i)

Canadian Tire "money," 94(i)

Card money, New France 4–10, 6(i), 7(i)

Central bank
    establishment (1934), 47–49
    Lord Sydenham's proposal, 21–22

Chartered banks
    advances to, under Finance Act, 38, 45n63
    bank note issues, *see* Bank notes
    failures in mid-1800s, 25
    impact of Bank Act (1871), 28, 28n45
    opposed to government notes, 22, 49

Coinage
    British (mid-1800s), 19(i), 27, 30
    Canadian, first issue (1858), 23(i), 24
    Canadian copper reorganized (1870), 31–32
    Canadian gold coins, 33(i), 41(i)
    Canadian silver coins, 31
    Dominion of Canada first issue (1870, 1876), 31–32, 32(i)
    minting, 24n35
    of New France, 3–10
    Province of Canada cent (1858), 23(i)
    ratings/values (pre-1841), 11–14
    removal of U.S. and British silver coins (1868–70), 28–32
    Spanish dollars, 4, 11
    Spanish 8-*real* piece (1779), 11(i)
    U.S. gold pieces, 21(i), 41
    U.S. half-dollar, 19(i)

Collins, John (editorial cartoon), 78(i)

Colonial Bank, 25

Colonial period, currency
    in British colonies (to 1841), 11–20
    in New France (1600–1770), 3–10
    reforms (1841–71), 21–32

Commodity prices, effect on dollar, 42

Community money, 95–96, 96(i)

Confederation, impact on currency, 22, 26–28

Consumer price index (CPI), 91

Copper shields, Haida, 2(i)

Copper tokens, 93

Coyne, James, 56
    disagreement with government (1961), 66–68
    on floating exchange rate, 62

Creighton, James, 41, 44

Currency, Canadian
    in British colonies, 11–20
    decimal-based, 21–24
    dollar vs. sterling as legal tender, 19–20
    first Canadian currency, 24–25
    of First Nations, 1–2
    impact of Confederation (1867), 22, 26–28
    of New France, 3–10
    ratings (valuations), 11–14
    see also Canadian dollar; Coinage; Paper currency

Currency Act (1853), 23, 24, 27

Davis, Robert, 34

Decimalization of currency, 21–24

Deflation
    during Depression years, 44–45
    effect of Advance Rate (1920s), 40

de Meulles, Jacques, 5

Depression years (1930-39), 44–47

Diefenbuck, 66(i)

Discount Rate (Federal Reserve Bank, U.S.), 45, 45n62

"Dollar," origins of, 20

Dominion notes, 27, 27(i), 31(i), 33n52, 39(i), 41

Dominion Notes Act (1868), 27
    amendment (1915), 39
    British issue, 39, 40
    provincial note issues, 27
    repeal (1935), 49

Exchange controls
    foreign exchange controls (1939), 51, 53
    vs. floating exchange rate (1949–51), 58
    regulations revoked (1951), 63
    unofficial exchange market (1939–50), 58–60
    during World War II, 51, 53–55

Exchange Fund Account (1939), 53

Exchange Fund Act (1935), 51

Exchange market intervention (1998), 81

Exchange Rate Mechanism (Europe), 80

Exchange rates
    all-time high (Canadian vs. U.S., 1858–2005), 36
    all-time low (Canadian vs. U.S., 1858–2005), 97
    Canada/U.S./U.K., 27, 97
    Canada/U.S. (1862–79), 35–36
    Canada/U.S. (1914–26), 38
    Canada/U.S. (1926–39), 43
    Canada/U.S. (1939–50), 51, 59
    Canada/U.S. (1950–62), 63
    Canada/U.S. (1970–2005), 84
    Coyne affair (1961), 66–68

devaluation (1949), 60
exchange controls (1939–46), 51, 53–55
fixed (1962–70), 66–70
fixed during WWI, 33
floating (1950–62), 61–65
floating (1970–present), 71–73
foreign exchange controls (1939), 51, 53
under the gold standard, *see* Gold standard
"managed" flexible exchange rate regime
        (1961), 68–69
revaluation (1946), 56
unofficial exchange market (1939–50), 58–60
unofficial rate (1940s), 60
FECB (Foreign Exchange Control Board) (1939), 53–54
Federal Reserve Bank (U.S.)
    Discount Rate, 45, 45n62
    reciprocal facility with, 69n87
Finance Act (1914), 38
    repeal (1935), 49
    revision (1923), 40, 40n58
    suspension of gold standard, 38
First Nations, 1–2
Fixed exchange rates, 53, 63n78, 66–70
Fleming, Donald, 68
Flexible (floating) exchange rates, 61–65, 63n78,
    71–73
Floating exchange rates, 61–65, 63n78, 71–73
Foreign Exchange Acquisition Order (1940), 55
Foreign Exchange Control Act (1946), 53n70, 63
Foreign Exchange Control Board (FECB) (1939), 53–54
Foreign Exchange Control Order (1939), 53
Foreign Exchange regulations, revoked (1951), 63
Free Trade Agreement, 79
French colonial period, currency, 3–10

Friedman, Milton, 60, 74
"Funny money" (prosperity certificates), 94–95, 94(i), 95(i)
Gable, Brian (editorial cartoon), 80(i)
Galt, A.T., 25
George King note, Montréal (1772), 92(i)
Gold, export and import points, 33–34
Gold devices, 42
Gold dust, 16n25
Gold reserves
    backing Dominion notes, 27, 27n42, 33n52,
        41–42, 43
    in devaluation of 1949, 57–58
    and exchange controls, 58
    transfer to Bank of Canada (1935), 51n69
Gold standard
    1854–1914, 33–36
    abandonment by Canada and U.K., 43
    "effective" suspension (1929–31), 45
    and monetary policy, 33–34
    return to (1926), 40
    suspension (1914–26), 37–40
    suspension by U.S. during Civil War, 35–36
Gordon, Donald, 60
Government-issued notes
    Dominion notes, 27, 27(i), 31(i), 33n52,
        39(i), 41
    fiat currency recommended (1867), 34
    proposals in 1841, 21–22
    Province of Canada notes, 24–26
    Treasury notes, 7, 8, 15–16
Grains (measures of weight), 13n23
Greenbacks (U.S.), 35–36, 35(i)
Gresham's Law, 8, 9

Halifax rating (of currency), 13–14
Hincks, Sir Francis, 22, 30
Home Bank, note, 38(i)
Hume, David, 10n14
Hyde Park Agreement (1941), 56

IMF (International Monetary Fund), *see* International
    Monetary Fund (IMF)
Inflation
    in Canada, 89
    in late 1960s, 71
    in mid-1970s, 75
    in New France, 6, 9
Inflation calculator, 88n1
Inflation targets, 80
Interest Equalization Tax (U.S., 1963), 70, 72
Interest rates, Can/U.S./U.K. (1914–2005), 98
International Bank, 25
International Monetary Fund (IMF)
    encouraged fixed rate (1970), 73
    establishment of, 65
    "managed" flexible exchange rate regime
        (1961), 68–69
    reaction to floating exchange rate, 64–65

Johnson, Harry, 86

Keynes, John Maynard, 40n57, 65
King, William Lyon Mackenzie, 52(i)

Laidler, David, 86, 87
Legal tender
    in 1926, 41
    British and U.S. gold coins, 23, 27, 41

Canadian gold coins, 41
chartered bank notes (until 1926), 37
colonial period (1841–67), 23
colonial period (to 1841), 15
definition, 2n3
discounted U.S. silver coins (1870), 31
Dominion notes, 27
non-convertible U.S. "greenbacks," 35–36
provincial notes, 24–26
Treasury notes, 7, 8, 15–16
Leman, Beaudry, 47, 47n67, 48
Lender of last resort (1914), 38
Long-Term Capital Management (LTCM), 82, 82n93
Louvre Accord (1987), 78, 79

Mackenzie, William Lyon, 95
MacKinnon, Bruce (editorial cartoon), 82(i), 83(i)
Mackintosh, W.A., 60
Macmillan, Lord, 47
Macmillan Report, 47, 48(i)
Macpherson, Duncan (editorial cartoon), 67(i), 69(i), 76(i)
Mallet, Louis, 5n7
Manitoba, decimalization (1870), 24
Marshall Plan, 61
Merchant token, 93(i)
Mexican peso crisis (1994–95), 80
Mills, 27
Monetarism, 74
Montcalm, Marquis de, 9

Monetary policy,
    in 1970s, 75
    in 1980s, 79
    during the Depression, 44–45, 47

exchange-market intervention (1998), 81
    under the gold standard, 33–34
    non-active oversight by government, 38
    restrictive vs. expansionary, 66, 67, 71
    during WWI, 38–40
Monetary targets, introduction of, 74, 75, 77
Montreal Bank, note, 16(i)
Moore, Marie, 5n7
Moral suasion, 74
    to protect gold reserves, 42, 43
    to reflate economy (1932), 45

National Energy Program, 77
New Brunswick
    currency, pre-Confederation, 15, 18, 18(i)
    currency legislation, 23
    decimalization (1860), 24, 24(i)
    Treasury notes, 15
New France (French colonial period)
    card money, 4–10, 6(i), 7(i)
    currency, 3–10
Newfoundland
    decimalization, 24, 24(i)
    pre-Confederation bank notes, 18
    provincial currency to 1895, 27n44
Northland Bank, 78
Notes, privately issued (New France), 7
Nova Scotia
    currency, pre-Confederation, 15, 18, 20
    decimalization (1860), 24, 24(i)
    provincial currency to 1871, 17(i), 27, 27nn43, 44
    Treasury notes, 15–16
Office of the Inspector General of Banks, 38(i)

Ordonnances, 7, 8(i)
Osborne, J.A.C., 49
Ottawa Mint, 24n35

Paper currency
    Army bills (1813), 14(i), 15
    card money, New France, 4–10, 6(i), 7(i)
    Dominion notes, 27, 27(i), 31(i), 33n52, 39(i), 41
    issued by chartered banks, 17–19
    issued by Province of Canada, 24–26
    proposed government issue, 21–22
    Treasury notes, 7–8, 15–16
    see also Canadian dollar; Currency, Canadian
Paper scrip (alternative money), 92
Parti Québécois and the Canadian dollar, 75
"Pence," origin of 20
Plaza Accord (1985), 77, 78
"Political currency," 66(i)
"Pound," origin of, 20
Price-specie flow, 34
Prices and Incomes Commission (1968), 71
Prince Edward Island
    currency, pre-Confederation, 18
    decimalization (1871), 24
    Treasury notes 15(i)
Prosperity certificates (alternative money, 1932),
    94–95, 94(i), 95(i)
Province of Canada (1841)
    coinage, 21, 23(i), 29
    government-issued notes, 24–26
    U.S. silver coins accepted at par, 29–31
Provincial Notes Act (1866), 26

Quebec
      currency, pre-Confederation, 3–10
      Parti Québécois government and the dollar, 75
      referendum (1980), 77
Quebec rating, 13n24

Racey, Arthur (editorial cartoon), 46(i)
Rasminsky, Louis, 64n79, 65, 68
Ratings (value of currency)
      colonial period, 11–14
      standardized, 12–13
Real (Spanish coin) (1779), 11(i)
Reid, Bill, 83(i)
Reidford, James (editorial cartoon), 72(i)
Routh, Sir Randolph, 20
Royal Bank of Canada, note, 54(i)
Royal Canadian Mint, 24n35

Salt Spring Island dollars (community money), 95–96, 96(i)
Saunders, J.C., 44
Seigniorage, 22n33
"Shillings," origin of 20
Shinplasters, 31, 31n51, 93
Silver nuisance, 28–31
Shortt, Adam, 3, 20
Smithsonian Agreement, 73
Spanish currency
      legal tender in colonial period, 4, 11
Stagflation, 74
Sterling
      currency in colonies, 11–20
      legal tender in Canada, 21, 23
      valuation of gold sovereign, 21n31, 23

Strong, Benjamin, 45
Sydenham, Lord, 21–22
Tingley, Merle (editorial cartoon), 89(i)
Tokens, brass and copper (alternative money), 93, 93(i)
Towers, Graham, 49, 52(i)
Trade silver, 3(i)
Trade tokens, 93
Treasury Board, and monetary policy, 40
Treasury notes, issues, 7, 8, 15–16
Trudeau just-a-buck (1972), 75(i)

Uniform Currency Act (1871), 27
United Kingdom
      gold standard, abandonment (1931), 43
      gold standard, suspension and return, 37, 40
United Kingdom, currency
      coinage (mid-1800s), 27
      gold coins, legal tender in Canada, 41
      silver coins in Canada, 30
United States
      capital outflow controls (1963), 70, 70nn88, 89
      gold exports during Depression, 45
      gold standard (Civil War), 35–36
      gold standard, suspension and return (WWI), 40
United States, currency
      gold coins, legal tender in Canada, 41
      gold eagle pieces, 21(i), 27
      greenbacks during Civil War, 35–36, 35(i)
      half-dollar (1853, 1859), 19(i), 28(i)
      quarter dollar (1827, 1859), 28(i)
      silver coins at par in Canada, 29–31
Upper Canada, ratings of currency, 14

Valuations, *see* Ratings
Vancouver Island colony, 24, 24n37
Victory Bonds, 37(i)

Wampum, 1–2, 1(i)
War savings stamp booklet (1940), 54(i)
Weir, William, 30, 30(i)
Weir tea service, 31(i)
White, Sir William, 47, 47n67
Winnipeg Agreement (1972), 74
World War I, gold standard, 37–40
World War II
        Canadian dollar in, 53–55
        exchange controls, 51, 53–55

Young, George, 12n20
York rating (of currency), 14

Zimmerman Bank (Bank of Clifton), 25, 25(i)